ENGLISH TABLE GLASS

EIGHTEENTH CENTURY GLASSES.
Typical Examples of the Five Main Groups.

2. Plain Stem.
   Height, 6½ inches.
4. White Twist Stem.
   Height, 6⅞ inches.

1. Baluster Stem.
   Height, 6¾ inches.

3. Air Twist Stem.
   Height, 6⅛ inches.
5. Cut Stem.
   Height, 6 inches.

ENGLISH TABLE GLASS

BY PERCY BATE

JM
CLASSIC EDITIONS

This edition digitally re-mastered and
published by JM Classic Editions © 2007
Original text © Percy Bate 1910

ISBN 978-1-905217-43-4

All rights reserved. No part of this book subject
to copyright may be reproduced in any form or
by any means without prior permission in writing
from the publisher.

To
MARY BATE

You planted the seed
  So the blossom's your own:
Be it flower, be it weed
You planted the seed,
If it please you to read
  You will see how it's grown—
You planted the seed,
  So the blossom's your own!

CONTENTS

CHAPTER		PAGE
	LIST OF ILLUSTRATIONS	ix
I.	INTRODUCTORY AND PREFATORY	1
II.	GLASSES OF THE SIXTEENTH AND SEVENTEENTH CENTURIES	20
III.	EIGHTEENTH-CENTURY GLASSES: THEIR NUMBER AND CLASSIFICATION	24
IV.	WINE GLASSES: BALUSTER STEMS AND PLAIN STEMS	33
V.	WINE GLASSES: AIR-TWIST STEMS	39
VI.	WINE GLASSES: OPAQUE WHITE AND COLOURED TWISTS—COLOURED GLASSES—CUT STEMS	48
VII.	ALE GLASSES AND OTHER TALL PIECES	58
VIII.	GOBLETS, RUMMERS, CIDER, DRAM, AND SPIRIT GLASSES	65
IX.	CANDLESTICKS, DECANTERS, SWEETMEAT GLASSES, TRAILED PIECES, ETC.	74
X.	METHODS OF DECORATION	81
XI.	FRAUDS, FAKES, AND FORGERIES: FOREIGN GLASS	88
XII.	INSCRIBED AND HISTORIC GLASSES	96
	INDEX	123

LIST OF ILLUSTRATIONS

With the exception of the four glasses figured on Plate LI, which are forgeries, all the illustrations without initials after their number in this list are from the collection of the author. The initials indicating ownership are to be read as follows:—

F.W.A.	=	Major F. W. Allan.
B.M.	=	British Museum.
J.T.C.	=	Mr. J. T. Cater.
P.	=	Dr. Perry.
R.P.	=	Mrs. Rees Price.

PLATE		TO FACE PAGE
I.	Eighteenth Century Glasses; Typical Examples of the five main groups: No. 1, Baluster Stem; No. 2, Plain Stem; No. 3, Air Twist Stem; No. 4, White Twist Stem; No. 5, Cut Stem	*Frontispiece*
II.	English Drinking Glass, A.D. 1586. Made in London by Jacob Verzelini B.M.	22
III.	Wine Glasses, Group I, Baluster Stems, Nos. 6, 7, 8, 9, 10	32
IV.	Wine Glasses, Group I, Baluster Stems, Nos. 11, 12 R.P., 13 R.P.	33
V.	Wine Glasses, Group I, Baluster Stems, Nos. 14 R.P., 15, 16	34
VI.	Wine Glasses, Group I, Baluster Stems with Domed Feet, Nos. 17, 18 R.P., 19, 20 R.P., 21 R.P.	35
VII.	Wine Glasses, Group II, Plain Stems, Nos. 22, 23 R.P., 24, 25, 26	36

ENGLISH TABLE GLASS

PLATE		TO FACE PAGE
VIII.	Wine Glasses, Group II, Plain Stems, Nos. 27, 28, 29, 30, 31 R.P.	37
IX.	Wine Glasses, Group II, Plain Stems with Domed Feet, Nos. 32 R.P., 33, 34 R.P., 35 . . .	38
X.	Wine Glasses, Group II A, Incised Twist Stems, Nos. 36, 37, 38 R.P., 39 R.P.	39
XI.	Wine Glasses, Group III, Air Twist Stems, Drawn, Nos. 40, 41 R.P., 42 R.P., 43 R.P., 44 R.P. . .	40
XII.	Wine Glasses, Group III, Air Twist Stems, Drawn, Nos. 45 R.P., 46 R.P., 47, 48 R.P.	41
XIII.	Wine Glasses, Group III, Air Twist Stems, Drawn, Nos. 49 R.P., 50, 51 R.P., 52 R.P. . . .	42
XIV.	Wine Glasses, Group III, Air Twist Stems, Drawn, Nos. 53, 54, 55, 56, 57	43
XV.	Wine Glasses, Group III, Air Twist Stems, Drawn, and with Domed Feet, Nos. 58 R.P., 59, 60, 61 R.P., 62 R.P.	44
XVI.	Wine Glasses, Group III A, Air Twist Stems, not Drawn, Nos. 63 R.P., 64 R.P., 65 R.P., 66 . .	44
XVII.	Wine Glasses, Group III A, Air Twist Stems, not Drawn, Nos. 67 R.P., 68 R.P., 69 R.P., 70 R.P., 71 R.P.	45
XVIII.	Wine Glasses, Group III A, Air Twist Stems, not Drawn, Nos. 72, 73, 74 R.P., 75 R.P., 76 . .	46
XIX.	Wine Glasses, Group III A, Air Twist Stems, not Drawn, Nos. 77 R.P., 78 R.P. ; Group III B, Mixed Twist Stems, not Drawn, 79, 80, 81 . . .	47
XX.	Wine Glasses, Group IV, White Twist Stems, Nos. 82 R.P., 83, 84 R.P., 85 R.P.	48
XXI.	Wine Glasses, Group IV, White Twist Stems, Nos. 86, 87 R.P., 88 R.P., 89, 90	50
XXII.	Wine Glasses, Group IV, White Twist Stems, Nos. 91, 92 R.P., 93, 94, 95	51
XXIII.	Wine Glasses, Group IV, White Twist Stems, Nos. 96, 97 R.P., 98, 99, 100	52

LIST OF ILLUSTRATIONS

PLATE		TO FACE PAGE
XXIV.	Wine Glasses, Group IVA, Coloured Twist Stems, Nos. 101 R.P., 102, 103, 104, 105	54
XXV.	Wine Glasses, Group V, Cut Stems, Nos. 106, 107, 108, 109, 110	55
XXVI.	Wine Glasses, Group V, Cut Stems, Nos. 111, 112 R.P., 113 R.P., 114 R.P., 115	56
XXVII.	Ale Glasses, etc., Baluster Stems, Nos. 116, 117 R.P., 118	58
XXVIII.	Ale Glasses, etc., Plain and Air Twist Stems, Nos. 119, 120, 121	60
XXIX.	Ale Glasses, etc., Air Twist and White Twist Stems, Nos. 122 R.P., 123, 124 R.P.	61
XXX.	Ale Glasses, etc., Air Twist and Cut Stems, Nos. 125 R.P., 126 R.P., 127	62
XXXI.	Goblet, Baluster Stem, No. 128	64
XXXII.	Goblet, Baluster Stem, No. 129	65
XXXIII.	Goblet, Drawn Stem, No. 130; Liqueur Glass, Drawn Stem, No. 131	66
XXXIV.	Rummers, Four Types of Stems—Plain Stem, No. 132; Air Twist Stem, No. 133; White Twist Stem, No. 134; Cut Stem, No. 135 R.P.	67
XXXV.	Two Handled Cup, No. 136; Rummers, Nos. 137 R.P., 138	68
XXXVI.	Rummers, etc., Nos. 139, 140 R.P., 141 R.P.	69
XXXVII.	Mugs or Tankards, Nos. 142 R.P., 143 R.P., 144	70
XXXVIII.	Yard of Ale Glass, No. 145, and Dram Glasses, Nos. 146 R.P., 147, 148, 149	71
XXXIX.	Dram and Spirit Glasses, Nos. 150, 151, 152, 153, 154, 155 R.P., 156	72
XL.	Dram and Spirit Glasses, Nos. 157, 158, 159, 160, 161, 162, 163, 164	73
XLI.	Candlesticks, Nos. 165 R.P., 166 R.P., 167 R.P.	74
XLII.	Toddy Fillers, Nos. 168, 169; Decanter, No. 170	75
XLIII.	Decanters, etc., Nos. 171, 172 J.T.C., 173	76

ENGLISH TABLE GLASS

PLATE		TO FACE PAGE
XLIV.	Sweetmeat Glasses, Nos. 174, 175, 176	77
XLV.	Sweetmeat Glasses, Nos. 177 R.P., 178 R.P., 179 R.P.	78
XLVI.	Sweetmeat Glass, No. 180 R.P.; Bell with trailed decoration, No. 181	79
XLVII.	Covered Bowl with trailed decoration, No. 182 R.P.	80
XLVIII.	Porringer with trailed decoration, No. 183	81
XLIX.	Methods of Decoration, Nos. 184 R.P., 185 R.P., 186 R.P., 187, 188, 189, 190, 191, 192	82
L.	Glasses decorated by means of fluoric acid, Nos. 193 B.M., 194 B.M.	86
LI.	Forgeries, Nos. 195, 196, 197, 198	89
LII.	Inscribed Glasses bearing Jacobite mottoes and emblems, Nos. 200 P., 201, 202	98
LIII.	Inscribed Glasses bearing Jacobite mottoes and emblems, Nos. 203 R.P., 204 R.P., 205 R.P.	100
LIV.	Inscribed Glasses bearing Jacobite mottoes and emblems, Nos. 206 B.M., 207, 208	101
LV.	Inscribed Glasses bearing Jacobite mottoes and emblems, Nos. 209 B.M., 210, 211 R.P.	102
LVI.	Inscribed Glasses bearing Jacobite and loyal mottoes and emblems, Nos. 212 R.P., 213 B.M., 214	104
LVII.	Inscribed Glasses bearing loyal and patriotic emblems, Nos. 215, 216, 217, 218	106
LVIII.	Inscribed Glasses commemorating national heroes, etc., Nos. 219 R.P., 220, 221	108
LIX.	Inscribed Glasses commemorating national heroes, etc., Nos. 222, 223 R.P., 224	109
LX.	Inscribed Glasses bearing political and social mottoes, etc., Nos. 225, 226 R.P., 227 J.T.C., 228, 229 B.M., 230 F.W.A.	110
LXI.	Inscribed Glasses bearing social mottoes and toasts, Nos. 231, 232, 233, 234, 235 F.W.A.	112

LIST OF ILLUSTRATIONS

PLATE		TO FACE PAGE
LXII.	Inscribed Glasses bearing the arms and motto of The Turners' Company of London, No. 236	113
LXIII.	Inscribed Glasses bearing social mottoes and emblems, Nos. 237 R.P., 238, 239, 240 R.P.	114
LXIV.	Inscribed Glasses bearing social and naval mottoes and emblems, Nos. 241, 242 R.P., 243 R.P.	116
LXV.	Inscribed Glasses bearing naval toasts and designs, Nos. 244, 245, 246, 247 .R.P	117
LXVI.	Inscribed Glasses bearing owners' names and allusive designs, Nos. 248, 249 B.M., 250, 251	118
LXVII.	Inscribed Glasses bearing pictorial emblems and mottoes, Nos. 252, 253, 254	120

ERRATA

The Drinking Glass on Plate II is not numbered.

No. 199 does not appear, but no illustration has been actually omitted.

ENGLISH TABLE GLASS

THE FIRST CHAPTER

INTRODUCTORY AND PREFATORY

LD English glass—which to all intents and purposes is the glass of the eighteenth century—has many interesting features and individual beauties. It lacks, as a whole, the fragile delicacy and the infinite variety of manipulation that characterize the products of the Venetian glass-houses; it is not marked by the florid decoration of enamels and gilding that is so typical of German work, nor do we find the English makers producing those lofty pieces, elaborately designed and somewhat redundantly engraved, that one associates with the Low Countries; but, as a whole, the glass vessels of the eighteenth century in England (and more particularly the drinking vessels) possess in their variety and their simplicity an interest which, though less clamant than that of their

ENGLISH TABLE GLASS

foreign congeners, is very real and very lasting.

And, apart from their intrinsic beauty and merit, they have for collectors of moderate means the advantage of being obtainable at a comparatively small cost. It is true that the last fifteen or twenty years have seen the prices asked by dealers increase by a hundred per cent., in response to the revived interest displayed in them by connoisseurs; and it is to be feared that these prices are not yet at their highest. But English glasses are still within the means of the buyer who cannot afford the porcelain of Chelsea or Worcester, of the lover of the art of a dead century to whom the silver of Paul Lamerie, or the miniatures of Richard Cosway, are things enviously to be foregone because of the unholy cost of them in the markets of the opulent.

It is for such friends of the arts of their own country as these that this book has been undertaken, in the expectation that some of those who feel the individuality of our English drinking glasses, respond to their charm, and care to possess them, may be interested in the experience and the

Increasing Interest of Collectors.

INTRODUCTORY AND PREFATORY

conclusions of a fellow-collector. That there is an increasing number of these there is no doubt; the artistic magazines (as well as the more "shoppy" periodicals) have recognized this fact, and have done much to foster the growth of this appreciation; and this renewed interest in the artistic products of the dead craftsmen of our own country is very pleasant to observe, and very welcome. For it can scarcely be denied that we have recently been rather apt, in the increasing recognition accorded to the art of others—the enamels of Japan and the terra-cottas of Tanagra, the lace of Flanders and the porcelain of Meissen—to overlook or dismiss slightingly the claims of our own simpler relics of the past.

Thomas Carlyle, that old philistine, defamed the dead years when he said of the eighteenth century that it was "massed up in our minds as a disastrous, wrecked inanity, not useful to dwell upon;" and it was reserved for a later historian to sound a truer note of characterization in speaking of that "century, so admirable and yet so ridiculous, so amusing, so instructive, so irritating, and so contemptible, so paradoxical and contradictory, *The Wonderful Eighteenth Century.*

ENGLISH TABLE GLASS

so provokingly clever, and so engagingly wicked." To-day that fascinating period, that cycle of mingled sincerity and artificiality, is receiving its true meed of appreciation, and is recognized as a time of golden fruition in the arts. English pictures of the period, and the contemporary miniatures and mezzotints, are rightly acknowledged as unsurpassed in their own way; the furniture, the porcelain, and the silver of that date are esteemed at their real value; and it is surely not too much to expect that the work of the craftsmen, who wrought in a more fragile, but not less beautiful material, and who produced the glass of the same period, should receive a little attention.

It is true that it is not possible, as it is in the case of silver and porcelain, to attribute any particular piece to an individual artist, or even to a recognized place of manufacture. The fragility of these little objects is mocked by the enduring strength of silver, their simplicity by the elaborate decoration possible to porcelain; but they have a charm all their own, nevertheless. The native quaintness and solid dignity of the forms of these English glasses, as well as the beautiful pellucidity of the material itself, would alone

INTRODUCTORY AND PREFATORY

constitute reasons for admiration, were there not the additional fact to be borne in mind that the untutored good taste of the unknown craftsmen who made these modest vessels, for use and not for ornament, saved them from the meretricious extravagances and decorative falsities that characterize a good deal of the work of the designers of furniture, silver, and china; just as the inherent tendency of molten glass to fall into simple and perfect forms assisted very largely to prevent any attempt at the production of types either fussy, bizarre, or grotesque.

For my own part, my attention was first drawn to the English glasses of the eighteenth century when I was shown some while on a visit to a beautiful old Georgian house in Mid-Sussex. *Beginning of the Author's Collection.* Here the fine old ale glasses, the interesting glass spoons with coloured twists in the handles, the quaint "wrythen" glasses for cordial waters, the simple wine glasses of brilliant metal, were family relics, most of them having been brought from the old haunted house at Pevensey, that was built by Andrew Borde (Merry Andrew), the physician to King Henry VIII, and inhabited by the forebears of my hostess almost ever

ENGLISH TABLE GLASS

since. These charmed me at the time, and on subsequent visits my interest in them did not diminish, indeed, it rather increased; and it always seemed to me that one of the quaintest of all was the old "drawn" glass, dating back to the middle of the eighteenth century, which was traditionally used, year in and year out, by the old folk on Good Friday. On this day, as the time between the morning and afternoon services was but brief, exhausted nature was sustained by each member of the family partaking of a mouthful of gingerbread and this glass full of gin. Later, when the elder daughter of the house was persuaded to assume control of my collection as well as of myself, she brought this glass with her to add to my cabinet, and to be treasured as the *fons et origo* of my hobby.

But before this happened, I had settled in Bath, and there, in the country that owned Bristol as its commercial capital, I found these quaint and beautiful glasses fairly plentiful. Gradually I bought examples, and though for a long time I could frame no sequence for them, they were very charming objects to possess. And then the beauty of the material, the

"The Accretion Fever."

INTRODUCTORY AND PREFATORY

delight that glass has for its lovers, began to take possession of me; and a piece or two of Venetian, some Dutch examples, a specimen of the Spanish, began to appear on my shelves, until I was brought up with a round turn by my good friend Mr. Drane, of Cardiff. He said, "I observe in you the symptoms of the 'the accretion fever,' the desire of acquiring, vaguely and without plan, for the mere sake of possession. You have neither money nor opportunity to form a collection of European glass; if you work on these lines you will never even get a representative group of English wine glasses. Drop the foreign gentry, and confine your energies to those of our own land. It is better far to have the best collection of English glass, or, at any rate, a collection in which every piece means something and fits into its place, than a mere meaningless aggregation, lacking coherence or antiquarian value."

This was very sound advice, and luckily I followed it. I am not, nor shall I ever be, the owner of the finest cabinet of English glasses; but I do possess a collection in which every piece fits into its place, and bears a relation to its neighbour, while illustrating some point of development or fashion.

ENGLISH TABLE GLASS

All growth is interesting, and all change, whether in the direction of development or **Fashion, Change, and Development.** of reaction; and few things are more attractive to the student of past days than the progress, the fluctuations, and the vagaries of fashion as illustrated in the changing forms and materials of household utensils. In tracing, for instance, the development of that simple object, the spoon, from the days of the fourth Edward to those of the fourth William, it is possible to see the influence of politics and religion, as well as the natural growth and evolution of the spoon itself. Here is the early "diamond point" that tops the shaft, changed later into the national acorn; here is the "slip-end" or so-called "Puritan" spoon, lacking the patron saint or apostle beloved in earlier days. Close by can be seen the fashion that came in with Charles II, supplemented by the one that followed with the Hanoverians; here a provincial maker, ignorant or conservative, continues to work by the old patterns long after they are out of fashion in London; there some innovator, greatly daring, shows the first step towards a new style.

All this, and much more, can be clearly

INTRODUCTORY AND PREFATORY

seen in such a collection of spoons as Mr. Drane himself possesses. Something similar, though of course less chronologically exact, and extending through a shorter period of time, may be observed in a series of the drinking glasses of the eighteenth century. It was not evident to me, as I said before, in the early days of my collecting, and for a long time I was working more or less in the dark, for there was not a single published volume, or even a magazine article, on the subject of my hobby. But slowly I evolved rules for my own guidance, learning a little from each piece that I acquired, and experiencing the great pleasure of seeing a sequence gradually arise, a series develop in which it became possible to see the gaps, to learn what to search for, and to fit the missing link when found.

And then came a chance notice of the comprehensive volume which was in preparation by Mr. Albert Hartshorne, F.S.A., and consequent correspondence, and later personal acquaintance with the gentleman who has made himself the admitted authority on the subject of English glasses. It is pleasant to me to think that I was able to

Mr. Albert Hartshorne and his Monograph.

assist Mr. Hartshorne with a few original observations and discoveries; it is still more pleasant to look back and recollect the invariable and unfailing courtesy and kindness with which he freely communicated to a beginner facts and deductions, information and advice, from his store of abounding knowledge and experience. His monumental volume, "Old English Glasses" (Arnold, 1897), must long remain, by reason of its elaborate completeness, the great authority on the subject; any such handbook as the present can but be an introduction to his encyclopædic treatment of the matter in all its ramifications; and those collectors who desire to learn the history of the craft of glass-making, and who wish for fuller information about our own English examples than I have space to convey, should consult Mr. Hartshorne's pages.

I have already spoken of the pleasure I derived from the growth of my small collection; the enjoyment obtained from the simple beauty of some, and the quaint originality of others; and the interest inseparable from the evolution of a series, the elucidation of little problems, and the development of a coherent story. This interest was, of course, both

Artistic and Human Interest.

INTRODUCTORY AND PREFATORY

artistic and antiquarian, but as yet the charm of the personal and individual was absent, though soon to appear. There is always to a thoughtful mind a curious fascination about those relics of the past that seem to touch, however faintly, the chord of human feeling, that seem to bear with them some suggestion, however slight, of the personality of the long dead men and women who possessed and cherished them in the bygone years. And gradually glasses came to my hand, frail relics of creed, or character, or emotion, which were eloquent of the ardent humanity of our predecessors, each with a tale to tell, each demanding hospitality and harbourage, and each affording either a vivid flash of insight or a half-veiled glimpse into the minds, the habits, and the identities of our ancestors.

What is more touching than constancy to a long-lost cause? What more rancorous than political hatred? From this glass, with its pathetic motto "*Redeat,*" some Jacobite drank, in secret and silence, to "the King over the water;" on this goblet we read the toast of "WILKES AND LIBERTY" daily pledged by some friend of freedom. And how human is our good old English sportsman TOM SHORTER, who has his name inscribed on his favourite glass, together with the pictured representation of himself "a-chasing the red deer" with horse and hound across the hills and combes of Exmoor; while what a tale, maybe of lifelong devotion, maybe of fleeting love, lies hidden in the name of some "dear, dead lady," some reigning toast, scratched with a diamond on the bowl of this other goblet. Here "TRAFALGAR" is commemorated; here the square and compasses tell of mysteries Masonic; here Admiral Byng, hanging from a gibbet, is falsely stated to have deserved "THE COWARD'S REWARD;" and so the tale might be continued. But sufficient has been said to show that, beyond the antiquarian value and the decorative charm of these old glasses, one finds in many the added interest always attaching to mementoes of deep feeling, to those slight and fragile objects, apparently foredoomed to early destruction, that have outlasted the often mighty and moving emotions of which they were but the passing outcome.

Collectors and Friends: Mr. J. W. Singer.

And over and above the pleasure that my glasses themselves have given me, there is the memory of the friendships they have brought and the delightful recollections associated with the acquisition of many of

INTRODUCTORY AND PREFATORY

them. It would be out of place to speak of all these here, even in a volume which is frankly of a personal (or rather a "first-personal") character, but allusion to one or two will, I am sure, be pardoned.

Early in the days of my collecting I came to know the late Mr. J. W. Singer, of Frome, the doyen of glass collectors and the kindest of friends. He had at that time, I fancy, ceased to collect very actively; but my enthusiasm revivified his own, and he once more began to seek for additions to his already large collection (it ultimately exceeded seven hundred), some few being acquired from myself, others direct from the dealers—a method very different from that of his early days. He has often told me how, as young men, he and a friend would take a pony-trap and drive round the country, inquiring at likely cottages if any old glasses "like that" (and they showed a specimen) were to be had. Often, of course, there was nothing; but often, too, excellent examples were acquired for a trifle; while sometimes the cottagers' glasses were but a memory, as in the case of the old lady who answered their inquiry with the provoking statement, " Law bless thee, zur! us had one o' they wi'

ENGLISH TABLE GLASS

a blue stem so long's my arm, but I broke en up wi' a hammer and put en down rats'-hole!"

To my hobby I am also indebted for many other pleasant acquaintances and friends. I confess that some of these owed to me their inoculation with the virus of the same collecting mania that I myself was a victim to (but they never seem to bear malice!); others, while immune from this particular form of the fever, viewed my own state with sympathy, and even fostered the progress of the malady by the gift of specimens. Many of the finest pieces I have I owe to the kindness of friends who have discovered, in travelling, examples not known to me; and these I mark in a certain way. It is a good habit to note on a small adhesive label on every piece the catalogue number, the date and place of acquisition, and the cost (the latter can be expressed by a private mark); and this I always do—unless I forget! But my price-cypher had no letter that stood for a gift, so I was driven to invent a symbol, with the consequence that all these presents from my very good friends (I do not forget to mark *them*) bear this emblem, ♡, in acknowledgment of the kind and generous hearts that have thus sought to give me pleasure.

INTRODUCTORY AND PREFATORY

When, some years ago, my work called me from Bath to Glasgow, I received in my new home no welcome more pleasant than that of Mrs. Rees Price, in whose cabinet of English glasses I found a collection much more numerous and varied than my own. From Mr. and Mrs. Rees Price I have received many tokens of friendship, but none that I value more than the very kind permission accorded me to draw with entire freedom on their examples for any photographs I needed for the illustration of this book; and I have not included more specimens from that source simply because the limits set by my publishers forbade the preparation of any more illustrations.

Mrs. Rees Price's Collection—and Others.

The mutual enthusiasm and the friendly and sympathetic rivalry between Mrs. Rees Price and myself still continue, and I hope will last for many years to come. My cabinet is the richer by her kindness; hers has a few additional specimens which might not be in her possession but for the good fortune which threw them in my way; and, though each has gaps not yet filled, the two collections taken together comprise a very adequate representation of the English glasses of the

ENGLISH TABLE GLASS

eighteenth century. It is for this reason (and the consequent simplification of the troublesome business of photographing the examples chosen for reproduction) that I have practically confined my illustrations to specimens chosen from Mrs. Rees Price's series and my own.

All glass collectors are good fellows, as a matter of course; and I am sure that other collections would have been placed at my service had I asked the favour. And I almost wish I had done so, if only to afford one more evidence of the kindly feeling and true courtesy induced by the cult of the same hobby. As it is, the owner of every glass illustrated is credited with the possession of the example in question, and I would beg all who have thus helped me to accept my sincere thanks.

The Illustrations.

In a volume such as this, in which an attempt is made to afford some slight guide to other collectors by the setting forth of one's individual experiences and conclusions, the illustrations must be of paramount importance. There is, of course, no method of learning the characteristics of any class of art objects at all comparable to that of personal inspection and handling; free access

INTRODUCTORY AND PREFATORY

to a fairly complete collection is the one desirable thing—whether the collection be pewter or porcelain, enamels or ivories—free access and the friendly talk of the collector. No book can take the place of this; but good photographic illustrations give a very fair idea of the appearance of the originals, and the author can endeavour to talk to his readers just as he would to a crony to whom he was displaying his treasures. And so I have assumed the post of guide, and, having taken the collections of Mrs. Rees Price and myself as being together fairly complete and representative, have selected with extreme care a thoroughly full and representative set of examples to be photographed for this volume, and have supplemented those when necessary from a few other sources.

The specimens thus illustrated in the first half of the volume will be found to make a series that lacks very few links, and with their aid, and that of the appended observations, it should be possible for the beginner to place any piece he may find. Should he come across any examples professedly of the eighteenth century, the prototypes of which

Typical and Individual Examples.

are not figured in these pages, he will do well to regard them with extreme caution; to treat them with suspicion even if he does not reject them; though at the same time it must be remembered that entire completeness and finality in cataloguing the glasses of this period has not yet been attained.

The examples illustrated in the second portion of the book have been selected on other grounds than the presentation of a historic sequence; they have been chosen because of their personal interest and their individual appeal. They are very interesting in themselves, and they will afford some guide as to the type of piece the industrious collector may hope, with good luck, to discover. It is, of course, in this group that the most elaborate and successful forgeries are produced; but of frauds, fakes, and spurious pieces there will be something to be said at a later stage.

All the illustrations (except some two or three as noted) are rather less than half the **Method of** height of the originals; for pur-
Photograph- poses of comparison the size of
ing Glasses. every piece has been given below its presentment.

As to the method of photographing, I have made many experiments, and have come

INTRODUCTORY AND PREFATORY

to the conclusion that none is so satisfactory as that employed to produce most of the figures in this book. I block up completely the middle light of a bay window, leaving the side lights clear, and about three feet in front of the centre light I place on a paper-covered surface the pieces to be taken, so that the light proceeds from behind the glasses on each side, and the illumination is even on both sides. By these means the best definition of any engraving on the bowl is secured, and each piece is clearly outlined against the dark background. Sometimes it pays, as in the case of the Jacobite glass (No. 200), to fill the bowl with a dark fluid to obtain the necessary definition of an inscription, but this is not, as a rule, desirable. There may be better ways of photographing glass, but I have seen no results produced by top, side, or front lights equal to those obtained by the illumination of the specimen from behind.

* * * * *

And now, after what has been, I fear, a sadly unconventional introductory chapter, I will take up my *rôle* of guide, and will embark upon an endeavour to present to my readers a coherent account of the glasses of the eighteenth century. Ladies and gentlemen, I crave your indulgence and your attention.

THE SECOND CHAPTER

GLASSES OF THE SIXTEENTH AND SEVENTEENTH CENTURIES

IN a volume such as this it is impossible to devote space, however much one would like to do so, to any history of the craft of glass-making in England. Our concern is rather with the actual glasses themselves; and of actual pieces which can be definitely assigned to English glass-houses prior to the closing years of the seventeenth century there are so few that it is almost hopeless to search for them, though they may as well be recorded here.

Mr. Hartshorne mentions three examples which may fairly be claimed as having been made in London in the reign of Good Queen Bess by one Jacob Verzelini, a Venetian, who worked in Crutched Friars under a patent for twenty-one years from December 15, 1575. One of these is known as Queen Elizabeth's glass, and is preserved in its leather case in the Royal collections at Windsor Castle; and another is the cylindrical glass tankard with silver and enamel mounts, preserved in the

English Elizabethan Glasses.

THE SIXTEENTH CENTURY

British Museum, the heraldry of which clearly shows that it belonged to William Cecil, Lord Burleigh. The third is the most interesting of the group, and is now also in the British Museum, by the courtesy of whose officials I am able to give two photographs of it (Plate II). It is a goblet covered with an elaborate decoration of scrolls and conventional ornamentation, which, with the inscription, has been executed with the diamond-point. The motto "IN : GOD : IS : AL : MI : TRVST" runs round the middle of the bowl, while in panels above are the date, 1586, and the initials G and S linked with a knot, the latter appearing twice. It is 5¼ inches high, and Mr. Hartshorne's attribution of it to Verzelini is, I think, incontrovertible.

It is always unsafe to express a decided opinion that any object of antiquity is unique, and it is not impossible that other glasses by Verzelini may be discovered. One, at any rate, has been found since Mr. Hartshorne's book was published, and was sent to a well-known London auction room for sale. It was a more important piece than the British Museum specimen, being 8 inches high, but was undoubtedly decorated by the same craftsman.

Another Piece by Verzelini.

ENGLISH TABLE GLASS

It bore the date 1584 (two years earlier than the other), and while the motto — running round the upper part of the bowl this time — was the same, letter for letter, the linked initials were M and W. But this splendid example was discovered only to be destroyed. It met with an accident at the auctioneers' rooms, being literally shattered to fragments, and I believe that the eminent firm who were entrusted with it paid the owner the rather extravagant reserve placed upon it, so terminating the history of one of the very few English Elizabeth examples extant.

Perhaps some collector who is searching for glasses of the eighteenth century may find yet another of the sixteenth, or, at any rate, one that purports to be of that date; but any such *trouvaille* must be regarded with extreme caution, for it has been suggested to me that the forger may be turning his unwelcome attention in this direction.

English Glass of the Seventeenth Century. Of the work of the "gentlemen glassmakers," immigrants from Normandy and Lorraine, who also set up glasshouses in Elizabethan times, no relic can be traced; nor is there any extant example which can be noted as the product of the various factories

PLATE 11

ENGLISH DRINKING GLASS.   A.D. 1586.   Made in London by Jacob Verzelini.
Height, 5¼ inches.

THE SIXTEENTH CENTURY

established in the earlier years of the seventeenth century under patents granted to Sir Jerome Bowes, Sir Edward Zouche, Sir Robert Mansel, and others. From the Duke of Buckingham's furnaces at Greenwich, where Venetian workmen were doubtless employed, the well-known " Royal Oak " glass probably came, and this may therefore be described as one of the few seventeenth-century pieces known. It is a square-shaped goblet, the bowl of which is elaborately decorated with a diamond-point, the decorations consisting of portraits of Charles II and his Queen, an oak tree bearing a medallion of the King, and a scroll inscribed " THE ROYAL OAK," and the date 1663. The metal is pale greenish brown, thin, very light, and devoid of brilliancy, lacking altogether the clear pellucid quality and the greater weight which half a dozen years later were to distinguish the native products from others made to English designs and requirements, and sent from Venice to the order of John Greene, citizen and glass-seller of London.

It is with these English rivals of the Venetian glasses, pieces dating from somewhere between 1680 and 1700, that we practically begin our native series.

THE THIRD CHAPTER
EIGHTEENTH-CENTURY GLASSES
THEIR NUMBER AND CLASSIFICATION

THERE is one of Charles Dickens' inimitable characters —was not his immortal name Wemmick?—to whose luminously deductive mind the sight of a church immediately suggested the necessity for a wedding; and similarly it would seem that the mere existence of a glass was, to our ancestors of the eighteenth century, at once a provocation and an inducement to use it—an attitude of mind admirably crystallized by the inscription on a glass belonging to Mrs. Rees Price, which proclaims itself (full or empty) as "BIBENDI RATIO."

Eighteenth-Century Habits. This habitual over-indulgence and insobriety has passed into history as one of the features of the epoch. It was a vice confined to no particular class; our Royal Princes were topers, and ministers of the Crown were not unaccustomed to the sight of two majestic

THE EIGHTEENTH CENTURY

figures in the Speaker's chair, where in sober moments they saw but one; and it is little wonder that men of a lower class continually " drank of the ale of Southwarke, and drank of the ale of Chepe," bemusing themselves without stint or stay. This undue liking for good liquor, so unhappily prevalent at that time in our country, was possibly one reason why so many glasses were made; the other, of course, was the increasing refinement and desire for luxury, which gradually pervaded those classes of society which previously had been content with a much coarser and ruder mode of life.

It is certain that in the eighteenth century drinking-glasses must have existed in their thousands, or there could not be, after the lapse of so many decades, such a number still extant. Prior to A.D. 1700, we know that comparatively little glass was made in our country, but about that date its manufacture seems to have greatly increased, for in A.D. 1696, Houghton (in his "Letters for the Improvement of Trade and Husbandry") records that there were eighty-eight glass-houses in England, at no fewer than twenty-seven of which the clear flint glass, so characteristically English, was made. From

ENGLISH TABLE GLASS

this time on glass of the finest quality was freely produced here, and the series of examples we have to consider may be taken to extend from A.D. 1690 to A.D. 1810, after which date our English glasses ceased to have decorative merit or individual value.

As a method of classification of the glasses of this period, it seems to me that **Method of Classification.** far the best plan is to make use of the five main groups into which the specimens themselves naturally fall when arranged according to the characteristics of their stems, especially as these groups coincide with the chronological sequence. Mr. Hartshorne supplements this with a more elaborate classification by the shapes of the bowls, while dividing the glasses as a whole into two main groups—the finer and the coarser (or tavern) examples. But though I am reluctant to discard the system of so eminent an authority, I fancy that the student will find that the stem classification alone is simpler and quite adequate. Indeed, the persistence of certain bowl-forms, right through the periods of development of at least three (and sometimes four) types of stems, seems to me to vitiate completely the utility of a classification by

METHOD OF CLASSIFICATION

bowls, which of necessity cannot be either chronological or evolutionary.

This arrangement by stems applies equally to goblets, tall ale glasses, small spirit glasses, and wine glasses, but as the latter are the most numerous, and form the completest series, I naturally commence with them.

The stems of these glasses, then, obviously fall into five groups, and these are illustrated in the frontispiece from good, simple, typical pieces. No. 1 may be called the *Baluster Stem*,* No. 2 the *Plain Stem*, No. 3 the *Air-twist Stem*, No. 4 the *White-twist Stem*, No. 5 the *Cut Stem*. **The Five Groups of Stems.** This is the chronological order of their appearance, and though all five groups had their side issues, so to speak, their offshoots and varieties, each was a real development from its predecessor, and every glass of the period will fall into one of these five classes. Of course it is not to be assumed that these five divisions succeeded each other without overlapping; indeed, the reverse is

---

* Mr. Hartshorne sometimes calls these "moulded," a term which seems likely to lead to confusion. They were not made in a mould, though some few of them show designs impressed from a stamp.

quite the case. Cut stems appeared probably as early as A.D. 1760, while air-twists did not die out till after that date; and plain stems naturally showed great persistence, as being more simply made and more moderate in cost than the elaborate twist. Nevertheless, taking the glass of the century as a whole, these are found to be the five great successive groups.

Of the types of bowls and their varieties something will be said presently; in the mean time it may be well to devote a little attention to the feet, which are as characteristic

The Three Classes of Feet.

and as important as the stems, though there are but three main divisions. In the first and earliest group, the under edge of the foot is turned or folded back on itself all round, the fold being anything between a quarter and a half an inch wide; while in the centre, the place where the workman's pontil was snapped off when the glass was completed, shows as a rough and sharp-edged excrescence, which, once seen, cannot fail to be recognized. This folded foot is to be found almost invariably associated with baluster stems (*e.g.* Nos. 6 to 12), generally with plain stems (as in Nos. 22 to 30), sometimes with

STEMS AND FEET

air-twists (see No. 58), and I had almost said never with white twists or cut stems. But a few weeks before these lines were written I acquired an example of a glass with a white twist and a folded foot (No. 91) and Mrs. Rees Price another; and this fact conveys one more warning—if one were necessary—as to the unwisdom of saying that a certain thing "does not exist." The folded foot, therefore, possibly continued in occasional use to about A.D. 1670, but simply as a relic of a bygone fashion of manufacture.

In feet of the second class the fold has been abandoned, but the rough pontil mark is retained; while in the third this excrescence has been polished away on the wheel, leaving a very smooth saucer-shaped depression. **The Pontil Mark.** The second group perhaps dates from A.D. 1740 (an exact date is impossible to fix), and lasted, at any rate, up to 1830, if not later; while the advent of the last development, following the use of the cutting-wheel on the stems (Group V), practically coincides with the end of the eighteenth century, and if found on any other than the cut stem-glasses, is almost sufficient to make the amateur reject the piece as spurious.

ENGLISH TABLE GLASS

These feet are either conical or domed, the latter being much the more uncommon form; and while the shallow cone, or normal foot (as will be seen from the illustrations), lasted all through the century, the domed variety is only found in association with baluster (Plate VI), plain (Plate IX), and, very rarely, air-twist (Plate XV) stems. The stunted goblets, smaller at the lip than at the base of the bowl, with poor white twists set upon domed feet, belong to the Low Countries.

Bowl Types and Nomenclature. It is always unwise to endeavour to improve on any system of nomenclature or identification that has become currently accepted, unless, of course, it is crassly imperfect; and Mr. Hartshorne has evolved so adequate a series of names for the different bowl types that it would be both unwise and ungracious to make any attempt to supersede it. But I have ventured to supplement his list with a few names which I use myself to distinguish varieties, so that the final catalogue of normal forms runs as follows:—

Drawn, *e.g.* Nos. 23 and 40.
Bell, Nos. 50, 51, and 52.
Waisted Bell, Nos. 37, 38, and 49.
Straight-sided, Nos. 24 and 25.

BOWLS AND THEIR TYPES

Straight-sided rectangular, Nos. 26, 54, and 71.
Ovoid, No. 57.
Ogee, Nos. 27, 28, 97, and 99.
Lipped Ogee, Nos. 81 and 100.
Double Ogee, Nos. 72 and 73.
Waisted, Nos. 77 and 78.

These different types of bowls are not confined to wine glasses, for it will be seen from the plates that the bowls of ale glasses, rummers, and dram glasses fall into the same groups, varying from their smaller congeners in dimensions but not in design. Vessels without a stem, mugs, tankards, and tumblers, describe themselves, and need no such classification as wine and ale glasses; and flutes, yards, and other more or less fantastic forms do not seem to call for inclusion or description at this point.

There will be occasion for some further remarks on most of these types as we come upon examples of each in reviewing the series as a whole; but we may note here the tendency in most of them to expansion of the lip, so that when the glass is filled the wine offers a comparatively large surface to the air. The capacity of such glasses as No. 72 (double ogee), No. 90 (waisted), and No. 59

ENGLISH TABLE GLASS

(bell), is very small; was the top made wide so that the bouquet of each glassful should be more diffused and more adequately presented to the palate of the connoisseur who was to partake of it?

PLATE III

WINE GLASSES.   GROUP I.   BALUSTER STEMS.
6. Height, 6⅝ inches.   10. Height, 6 inches.   7. Height, 6½ inches.
8. Height, 6¼ inches.   9. Height, 6¼ inches

PLATE IV

WINE GLASSES. GROUP I. BALUSTER STEMS.
11. Height, 7⅝ inches. 12. Height, 7⅛ inches. 13. Height, 7½ inches.

THE FOURTH CHAPTER

WINE GLASSES

BALUSTER STEMS AND PLAIN STEMS

THE earliest glasses of the series, those which may approximately be said to date from A.D. 1680 onwards, are very heavy and lumpy, and far more odd than beautiful; and yet I confess that I have for them a particular partiality. These great masses of clear and brilliant metal at any rate possess character; and though the bowls are of such varied and out-of-the-way forms as to defy inclusion in any system of classification, they consort fitly with the quaintly designed stems, the whole (to me, at any rate) possessing something of impressiveness and something of sturdy dignity.

Group I: Baluster Stems.

In the series illustrated on Plates III, IV, V, and VI, the extreme thickness of the bases of some of the bowls and the prevalence of irregular bubbles of air (the so-called "tears") in the stems of the majority should be noted. These latter are not accidents, but constitute the earliest form of stem adornment. Later

ENGLISH TABLE GLASS

they develop into the air-twists, and in some cases they are large enough to enclose a coin. The presence of this coin (by the way) does not prove that the glass was made in the year of its mintage (it *may* be much later); it only proves that it cannot be earlier.

The only notable tendency to ornament in these glasses is exemplified in No. 10, a piece in which we may see on the shoulders of the stem small stars impressed in relief. Other like designs are similarly used, and in the second half of this book a glass bearing an inscription thus applied will be figured.

Notice should also be taken of the group in Plate VI of glasses of this period (somewhere between A.D. 1690 and A.D. 1740) with the domed feet already alluded to, the effect of which in these specimens is very pleasant; and a gradual refinement of outline and detail as the series develops also deserves attention.

There is no clear line of demarcation between Groups I and II, for the heavy **Group II:** baluster stem glasses figured and **Plain Stems.** noted above merged gradually into a simpler and lighter type. No. 63, for instance (associated with a later group

PLATE V

WINE GLASSES. GROUP I. BALUSTER STEMS
14. Height, 6½ inches. 15. Height, 7⅞ inches. 16. Height, 6⅞ inches.

PLATE VI

WINE GLASSES. GROUP I.
BALUSTER STEMS WITH DOMED FEET.

20. Height, 6 inches.
19. Height, 6½ inches.
21. Height, 6⅜ inches.
17. Height, 6 inches.
18. Height, 6⅞ inches.

WINE GLASSES

because of a comparison to be made when that series is reached), might equally justly, or even preferably, be classed as a baluster-stem type; but when we come to such pieces as No. 25 and No. 28 there can be no doubt as to what class they fall into. The folded foot is the almost invariable accompaniment of the plain stem, though sometimes, as in the pieces figured in Plate 9, the domed foot occurs, and the metal of many of these examples is of a faintly darker tint than that of the earlier and more massive pieces; but I do not know that any particular deduction can be drawn from this little fact.

No. 23 has been selected for illustration because its stem shows a very long and slender form of the "tear," the development from which of the simplest air twist is not difficult to see; others, in their knops and swellings on the stem, foreshadow the advent of the more elaborately formed stems that were to succeed them, No. 25, for instance, with its "high-shouldered" form—to me a very pleasing type. Possibly the earliest of this group is No. 27, with the curious hollow in the stem, almost too large to be called a "tear;" while No. 30, showing a very characteristic engraved border, comes late, although it possesses the folded foot; and perhaps latest of all is No. 31, with its particularly beautiful decoration of the natural rose in bloom (evidently cut by an artist and a master of his craft), which affords a sharp contrast to the simple convention for the same flower to be seen on Nos. 26, 27, and 29, the latter being a very frequent type to be found over a long series of years.

In this group we find the erratic bowl forms of earlier days replaced by certain of the accepted and permanent types. No. 2, the bell, is a type of bowl largely employed in the Low Countries (especially at a slightly later date in conjunction with white twists); while No. 24, the straight-sided, exhibits, on the other hand, a shape particularly English and very persistent, which is found up to the very end of the century; No. 28, the single ogee, is a form which it has been suggested was largely made at Bristol; and No. 23, the simple drawn form, is the forerunner of a very long series of glasses, many of great beauty and merit.

On an earlier page I have spoken of branches and offshoots from the main line of development, some of which are puzzling and difficult to place properly; and I now

PLATE VII

WINE GLASSES. GROUP II. PLAIN STEMS.
22. Height, 5⅞ inches. 26. Height, 6 inches. 23. Height, 6¼ inches.
24. Height, 6⅛ inches. 25. Height, 6⅛ inches.

PLATE VIII

WINE GLASSES. GROUP II. PLAIN STEMS.
28. Height, 5⅜ inches. 27. Height, 6¼ inches. 29. Height, 5⅞ inches.
30. Height, 5¼ inches. 31. Height, 5 inches.

WINE GLASSES

come to one of these little problems, in the shape of the early glasses which show on the outside of the stem an incised twist. Three of these are figured on Plate X, and it would not have been difficult to include others; indeed, Nos. 39 and 205 present this characteristic also, as does a comparatively short glass of the drawn form which is in my possession. But Nos. 39 and 205 must be clearly distinguished from the others, both as to date and metal, the latter showing a dark tinge (distinctly blue as contrasted with the normal white basic hue) and a certain streaky and bubbly consistency quite different from the usual clear colourless glass; while on Nos. 36, 37, and 38, the incised grooves are much further apart than on the others named. *Group II a: Stems with Incised Twist.*

No. 39 and its congeners are comparatively late, belonging to the middle of the century; but Nos. 36 and 38 are undoubtedly old, showing the folded foot and other signs of age (as does a similar piece in the cabinet of Mr. J. W. Singer). No. 37 is perhaps not so early, and has no fold; but I have yet another piece of this very form and metal, with a drawn air-twist stem, which *does* exhibit the folded foot. Does this imply that these glasses, uncommon as they are now, were made over a short period of years during which the fold went out of fashion? Did they all, with their characteristic twist, the curious waisted form of the bell bowl, and their dark metal, emanate from one early glass-house? Inasmuch as all the pieces I know were found in the west of England, I am inclined to think this suggestion not an impossible one.

Their method of manufacture was obviously as follows: a short stem would, while soft, be impressed lengthwise with parallel grooves; this would then be attached to the bowl, drawn out, and, during this process of lengthening, would be twisted, producing not only the outside spiral indentation, but also the thinness of the centre of the stems, which is quite noticeable in Nos. 36 and 38.

PLATE IX

WINE GLASSES. GROUP II.
PLAIN STEMS WITH DOMED FEET.
32. Height, 7⅛ inches. 33. Height, 6¾ inches. 34. Height, 6¾ inches.
35. Height, 6¼ inches.

PLATE X

WINE GLASSES.   GROUP IIA.   INCISED TWIST STEMS.

36. Height, 6 inches.   37. Height, 7 inches.   38. Height, 6 inches.
39. Height, 5⅞ inches.

THE FIFTH CHAPTER
WINE GLASSES
AIR-TWIST STEMS

IN some respects the glasses illustrated in Plates XI to XIX are the most beautiful of our English pieces, as they are in many ways the most characteristic. They possess a brilliance of metal which is enhanced by the silvery brightness of the spirals in the stems; their forms, being those naturally evolved from the simple and legitimate use of the material, are almost, without exception, graceful and refined; and the design and decoration of both bowls and stems leave little to criticize.

Group III: Air Twists: Drawn.

The air-twist stems fall into two groups: the first comprising those in which the stem was made in one piece with the bowl, being *drawn* from it in the process of manufacture, as is the case with the plain stems; the second consisting of the glasses which were made in three parts—bowl, stem, and foot.

In the second case the stems were first made in rods of some length, which were cut up into shorter pieces, each suitable for the

ENGLISH TABLE GLASS

stem of a glass, and the bowls and feet were welded to them; in the first group the twist **Method of Manufacture.** was formed by the workman introducing into the base of a partially made bowl small bubbles of air or "tears" (*cf.* No. 85), which, when prolonged and twisted, gave the charming effect exemplified in No. 42—to take a simple case—in which the effect is practically that of two such elongated "tears" as the one in No. 23, to which a spiral form has been communicated by twisting. No. 60 in Plate XV is another early and easily analyzed example.

These air twists are typically English; they were greatly in vogue, and their popularity lasted for a long time, probably at least as late as A.D. 1780; and they are generally associated with feet of the normal type possessing rough pontil marks. But Nos. 60, 61, and 62 exhibit domed feet, being probably the latest examples of this type we have; and No. 57, a singularly graceful and pure form, has the foot of the third type (with the pontil mark polished off), from which it may be concluded that it belongs to quite the end of the century.

The simple drawn form exemplified in Nos. 40 and 42, 43 and 44, with their varieties

PLATE XI

WINE GLASSES. GROUP III.
AIR TWIST STEMS—DRAWN.
40. Height, 6¾ inches. 42. Height, 6¼ inches. 41. Height, 6⅜ inches.
43. Height, 6⅞ inches. 44. Height, 7 inches.

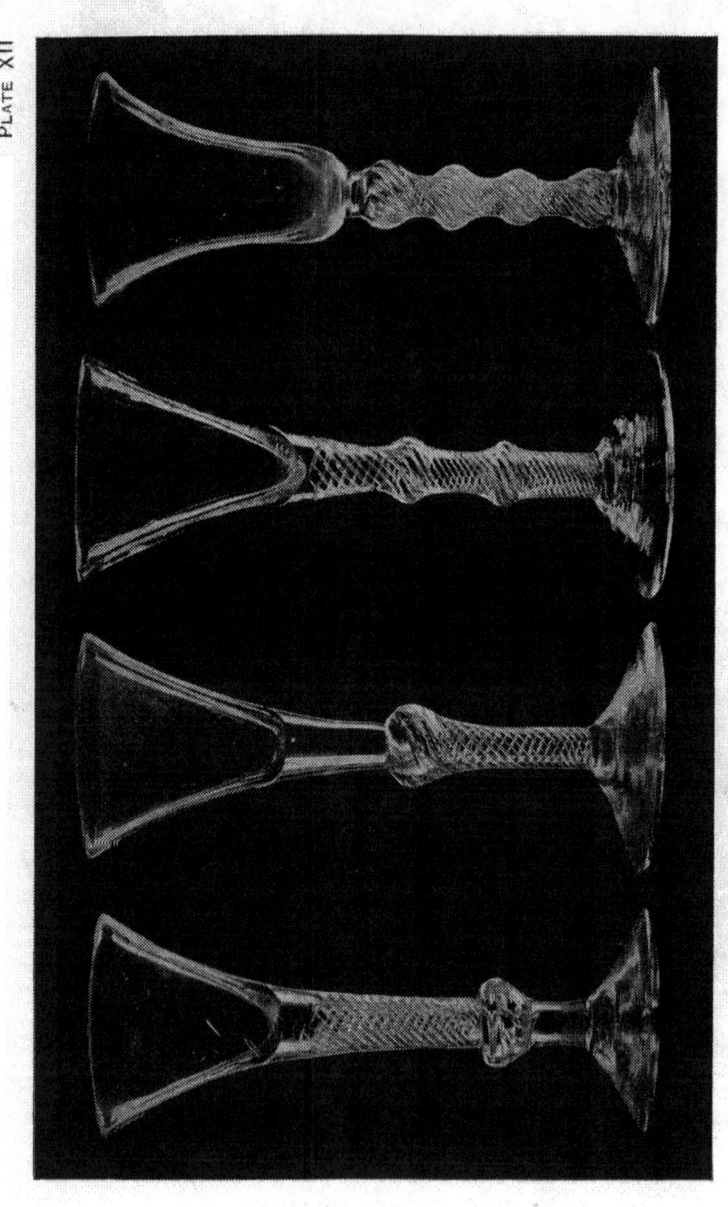

WINE GLASSES.   GROUP III.   AIR TWIST STEMS—DRAWN.
45. Height, 6⅞ inches.   46. Height, 7 inches.   47. Height, 7¼ inches.   48. Height, 6⅞ inches.

WINE GLASSES

of twist (each inviting close and careful examination), were succeeded by others. The bell bowl was a natural development, and a very interesting variety—the intermediate stage between the characteristic drawn form and the typical bell—is figured in No. 41 ; while of the bell form proper, Nos. 48 and 50, 51 and 52, are given as fine and representative examples. It is interesting to note how in No. 49, for instance, the twist starts in the bowl, and is uninterruptedly continued all down the stem ; and how in No. 51 a compressed neck causes a thinning of the air tubes, which becomes almost a complete elimination of them in No. 61 ; while in No. 52 and the following pieces, the spirals start below this neck. Examples exist, more marked in character even than No. 61, in which the formation of this neck has compressed the twist out of existence, leaving only a series of bubbles in the base of the bowl entirely separated from the threads in the stem.

Varieties and Types of Bowls.

Drawn air twists are also found with straight-sided and straight-sided rectangular bowls (see Plate XIV) ; but I have never seen them associated with ogee or waisted bowls,

ENGLISH TABLE GLASS

so whether these latter were made or not I cannot say. They appear, however, in the next group.

I have already alluded to the varieties of the air twist, each of which possesses an in-

Varieties of Twist and Stem.

dividual charm, and so shall not dwell on them further; but before leaving this group, I must briefly call attention to the pleasing variety of the knops or swellings on the stems (see Plates XII, XIV, and XV), which afford a welcome relief to the severer lines of the plain ones; and to the rare cable coil (which sometimes takes the form of a simple band or collar) placed round the shaft of No. 50. It has been suggested that these knops and collars were introduced to secure a safer grip of the glass for the gouty and otherwise unsteady fingers of habitual topers, but in view of the eighteenth-century fashion of holding and lifting the glass *by the base*, this seems doubtful.

The difference between the method of making the glasses of this group and those

Group III a: Air Twists, not drawn.

of the preceding class has been already noted, and whenever a cursory examination of typical pieces from each is made, the points

PLATE XIII

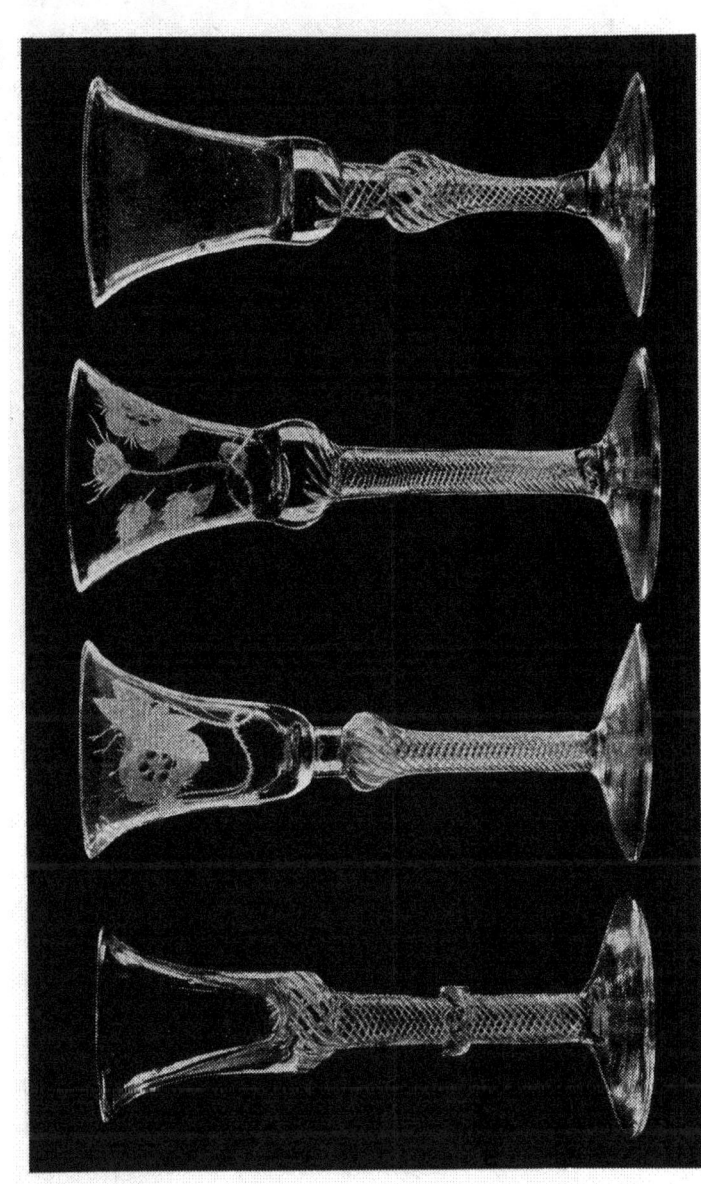

WINE GLASSES.   GROUP III.   AIR TWIST STEMS—DRAWN.
50. Height, 6⅞ inches.   52. Height, 7 inches.   49. Height, 7¼ inches.   51. Height, 6⅞ inches.

PLATE XIV

WINE GLASSES. GROUP III. AIR STEMS—DRAWN.
54. Height, 6¼ inches. **53.** Height, 6⅞ inches. **57.** Height, 5⅞ inches.
55. Height, 6¼ inches. **56.** Height, 6⅜ inches.

WINE GLASSES

of divergence cannot but be clear. But before turning to the added variety of bowls and twists to be found in this class, there are two glasses figured on Plate XVI which call for notice. The first is No. 65, which is more or less of a puzzle, and perhaps might just as correctly be included among the drawn twists, for the upper part of the stem was clearly made in that way; but the half below the knop would seem to be a portion of a length of stem separately made, and fitted into the lower side of the bulb just as the drawn portion was welded into its upper side. That these two halves are not parts of the same shaft, but two separate pieces joined at the knop, is obvious, if only from their complete lack of accurate alignment.

The other glass which is noteworthy is No. 64, and this piece must be alluded to for two reasons. The first is the curious perpetuation (possibly due to the innate conservatism of your British craftsman) of an earlier form—a form which almost belongs to the group of baluster stems, as will be seen on comparison with No. 63, a glass clearly of the latter class. The second point is that this stem, though joined to the bowl by a "collar," and not drawn from it, is

Persistency of Type.

ENGLISH TABLE GLASS

yet a *drawn* stem, being clearly made by that method in one piece with the foot: a fact quite evident if the figure be turned upside down, and the stem compared with those of No. 62 and its congeners. This "collar," by the way, is rather a prevalent feature of this group of glasses, and may be seen in Nos. 68, 69, 174, and 236.

It was obviously possible, when the stems were made separately, to evolve a greater variety of twists and spirals than when they were produced as part of the bowl; and the consequence is that the stems of this class are more elaborate than their forerunners, though it must be admitted that what was gained in richness in this way was often lost in beauty and suavity of outline and form. And it cannot fail to be noticed that, in addition to this increased richness of the stems, the bowls in this group are also more varied than in the preceding one. Though the drawn form is naturally absent, bells of two types are to be found, simple, as in No. 67; waisted, as in No. 68; while the straight-sided (No. 69), waisted (No. 78), single ogee (No. 80), the same, lipped (No. 81), and double ogee (the quaint and pretty shape so well exemplified

Varieties of Stem and Bowl.

PLATE XV

WINE GLASSES. GROUP III.
AIR TWIST STEMS—DRAWN, AND WITH DOMED FEET.

58. Height, 6⅞ inches.   **60.** Height, 7 inches.   **59.** Height, 6 inches.
61. Height, 6⅝ inches.   **62.** Height, 6⅞ inches.

PLATE XVI

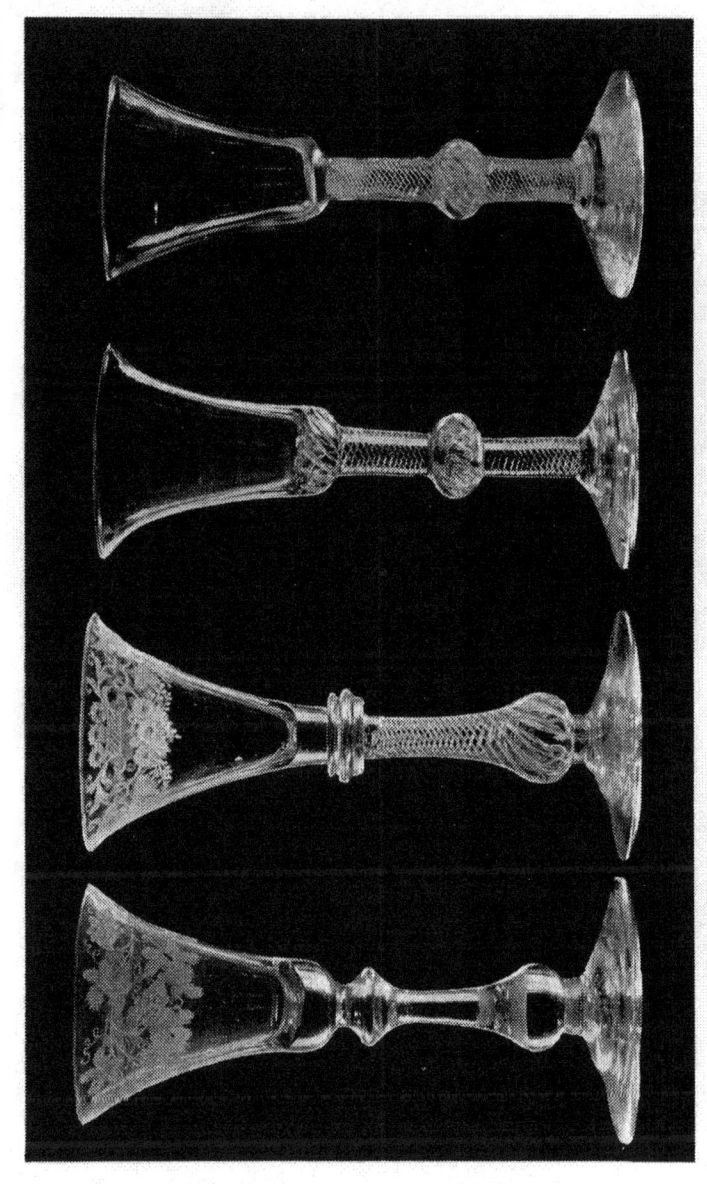

WINE GLASSES. GROUP IIIA. AIR TWIST STEMS—NOT DRAWN.
63. Height, $6\frac{7}{8}$ inches. 64. Height, $6\frac{3}{4}$ inches. 65. Height, $6\frac{5}{8}$ inches. 66. Height, $6\frac{1}{2}$ inches.

PLATE XVII

WINE GLASSES. GROUP IIIA.
AIR TWIST STEMS—NOT DRAWN.
67. Height, 6 inches. 68. Height, 6¾ inches. 69. Height, 5⅞ inches.
70. Height, 6⅛ inches. 71. Height, 6 inches.

WINE GLASSES

in No. 72), are all to be found. This is the first time this latter type appears among the illustrations to this book, but it exists with a plain stem of the character of No. 28, though neither Mrs. Rees Price nor I possess an example.

In glasses with air-twist stems occur also the ornamentation of the bowl by shallow perpendicular grooves (No. 80), and by a sort of raised reticulation (No. 70), as well as by the engraving which has been familiar in the preceding sections. In this connection the patterns of the engraving are worth attention — No. 62, a survival from earlier types; No. 41, with its pretty conventional rendering of a basket of flowers; No. 52, with its rose and moth; and Nos. 43 and 75 also, as excellent examples of their respective styles.

With the next class of stems we come to one of those little intermediate links that are so interesting and so delightful **Group III b:** to the student who is concerned **Mixed Twists.** with the evolution and fluctuation of design, for in the stems of mixed twists—twists, that is, which combine air threads and opaque white threads—we find the intermediate stage which fills the gap that would otherwise exist between the air twists proper and the white

ENGLISH TABLE GLASS

spirals. They are very uncommon, are found only in glasses of a good type, and exhibit a charming effect which is quite their own. The three examples reproduced from my own collection illustrate their details quite well, and although it is impossible to secure in a photograph a really fine rendering of the variation of the threads, it will be noticed that in No. 79 a single silvery air thread runs like a streak of mercury down the inside of the white coil; that in No. 80 the cluster of threads is composed of air twists, the alternating spiral and the centre thread being opaque white; and that in No. 81 two white flat tapes alternate with two flat air-twists.

Leaving now the great division of air-twist stems for that which comprises the opaque white spirals, there are two features that call for a final note: the pellucid white metal of which these pieces are made, and the almost invariable presence, in glasses with the air twist, of the second type of foot — that with the pontil mark. I have already commented on this latter point (p. 40), and noted that No. 57 has the polished foot, and I find that Mrs. Rees Price has two (not drawn) with the same feature; but these pieces are only the

Feet with Pontil Marks.

PLATE XVIII

WINE GLASSES. GROUP IIIa.
AIR TWIST STEMS—NOT DRAWN.
72. Height, 6 inches. 74. Height, 6½ inches. 73. Height, 6¼ inches.
75. Height, 6⅝ inches. 76. Height, 6½ inches.

PLATE XIX

WINE GLASSES. GROUP IIIA.
AIR TWIST STEMS—NOT DRAWN.
77. Height, 6¼ inches. 78. Height, 6¼ inches.

GROUP IIIB. MIXED TWIST STEMS—NOT DRAWN.
80. Height, 6⅞ inches. 79. Height, 7⅝ inches. 81. Height, 6 inches.

WINE GLASSES

exceptions that prove the rule, for there is no doubt in my own mind that they are belated survivals (reproductions, though not forgeries) belonging to quite the end of the eighteenth century, if not to the early years of the nineteenth.

THE SIXTH CHAPTER
WINE GLASSES
OPAQUE WHITE AND COLOURED TWISTS
COLOURED GLASSES
CUT STEMS

IT has been suggested that the glasses of the fourth group, those with opaque white spirals in the stems, may date from as early as A.D. 1745, and though no piece appears to exist which bears a date approximating to that, glasses of this type,
Group IV: White Twists. bearing dates from A.D. 1757 onwards, are known and recorded. It may perhaps be justifiably assumed that they were the vogue at about A.D. 1760, and that they lasted almost to the end of the century, the coloured twists which mark their latest stage of development appearing towards the end of their career, probably *circa* A.D. 1780.

I cannot do better than quote Mr. Hartshorne's description of the way in which these stems were made.
Method of Manufacture.
He says—

" A cylindrical pottery mould of about 3 inches high and 2½ inches wide was fitted around its interior circumference

PLATE XX

WINE GLASSES. GROUP IV. WHITE TWIST STEMS.

82. Height, 7 inches.
84. Height, 6½ inches.
83. Height, 4¾ inches.
85. Height, 7 inches.

WINE GLASSES

with a series of opaque white glass canes, alternating with rods of the same size in plain glass to keep them an accurate distance apart, all being further retained in place by a little soft clay in the bottom of the mould. This receptacle and its contents were then heated up to the point when melted glass might be safely introduced into the wide space in the middle. The hot canes adhering to the molten metal, the whole was then withdrawn from the mould, re-heated in the furnace, and the canes drawn together at one end by the pincers; the cylinder was now revolved and prolonged to the proper distance, and a twisted stem of the required thickness, of opaque white filagree, was the result. It is obvious that by varying the positions of the canes, opaque, coloured or plain, and manipulating as described, twisted rods of endless variety could be produced."

These rods were cut up into suitable lengths, and on to each length the bowl and foot were welded; so that it is obvious that in this group we find a method of construction entirely analogous to that employed with the air-twist stems of Group III A.

Knowing the method of making these stems, it is clear that it would be exceedingly difficult, if not impossible, to employ in the production of a glass with a white twist stem the method used to make the drawn glasses of earlier date; but Mr. Hartshorne illustrates a very rare and interesting piece, analogous in design to No. 49, in which the white

Do Drawn Opaque Twists exist?

49

ENGLISH TABLE GLASS

threads show the same change from perpendicular in the base of the bowl to spiral in the stem, as in the drawn bell glasses. It simulates the effect of No. 49 exactly, whether it was made in the same way or not; and should the amateur discover one of these, it is a piece to acquire, if only because it affords an interesting problem.

But though the "drawn" method of manufacture was not the method of the **English or** white twists, the drawn type of **Dutch.** glass was a popular one, and in Plate XX are a couple of examples (Nos. 82 and 83), and in Plate XXI another (No. 86), of white twist glasses which follow the drawn form; No. 83, by the way, being possibly rather a cordial water or spirit glass than a wine glass. Mr. Hartshorne is of opinion that these are all, without exception, the products of the Low Countries, and he places No. 84 in the same category; but it is difficult to see why every other type should be made in England (where the drawn air-twist glass was admittedly a favourite pattern, and where No. 84 can be almost absolutely matched in an air twist, *cf.* No. 48), and this not. No. 96, for example, is admittedly English, and so is No. 95, and the difference

PLATE XXI

WINE GLASSES. GROUP IV. WHITE TWIST STEMS.
87. Height, 6⅛ inches. 86. Height, 7⅝ inches. 88. Height, 6 inches.
89. Height, 6⅛ inches. 90. Height, 6⅛ inches.

PLATE XXII

WINE GLASSES. GROUP IV. WHITE TWIST STEMS.
91. Height, 5⅝ inches. 95. Height, 7⅝ inches. 92. Height, 5¾ inches.
93. Height, 6¼ inches. 94. Height, 6⅛ inches.

WINE GLASSES

between this last and Nos. 82 and 86, for instance, is simply one of degree and not of kind. Possibly we may conclude that this form, like the bell bowls illustrated in Nos. 84 and 85, is common to both countries, and we may admit, at the same time, that it is extremely difficult to distinguish between the English pieces and the foreign ones. The Dutch glasses are often of good metal and true ring, with twists of white as fine as our own; but others from Holland, less fine, are easily recognized, and will be alluded to later.

With the smaller glasses figured on Plate XXI we come to pieces that are indubitably English, as are those illustrated on Plates XX and XXIII. Here it will be better to turn to the forms of the bowls, leaving the multiplicity of twists and spirals to speak for themselves. Every one of these bowl shapes has been already found associated with air-twists, though in this group the plain ogee (of which Nos. 97 and 98 are such excellent examples) and the straight-sided are the most frequent. The ogee type is said to be largely the product of Bristol glass-houses, and this is not unlikely, for among the pieces coming from the west of England I have noticed many

Bowls: Ogee and Straight-sided.

ENGLISH TABLE GLASS

variants of this form, and many intermediate shapes insensibly merging into each other. Of the more strongly marked variants a few carefully selected examples are figured—the waisted form (No. 89) and the lipped piece (No. 100, which shows a raised mesh-like decoration at the base) being handsome in their way; while the piece with perpendicular corrugations (No. 99) is interesting to me personally, because it is the first glass I ever purchased.

Some of the straight-sided glasses also show these perpendicular ripplings (sometimes spirally twisted or "wrythen"), which give a lightness and brilliance of effect quite pleasing (No. 93, for example); and these develop into flutings, as in No. 92, which flutings were repeated in the cut bowls of the glasses of the early nineteenth century; while in rare cases we find two horizontal grooves (see No. 91) running round the bowl. This last type is not common, and it has been suggested that it emanates from a glass-house at Lynn or Norwich; and as both Mrs. Rees Price's example and my own (each, by the way, showing the *folded* foot) came from that district, the conjecture may reasonably be accepted.

PLATE XXIII

WINE GLASSES. GROUP IV. WHITE TWIST STEMS.
97. Height, 5⅞ inches. 96. Height, 7⅜ inches. 98. Height, 5⅞ inches.
99. Height, 6 inches. 100. Height, 6 inches.

WINE GLASSES

The waisted bowl (as No. 90) has already been noted among the air-twists, but this piece deserves a little attention, being quite charming in form and decoration; and the double ogee (No. 88) also occurs in Group III A. This double ogee form would at first sight seem to be a lipped development of the straight-sided glass, but No. 87 raises the interesting question as to whether it was not rather an offshoot of the drawn form. Whichever it may be, it is a pretty shape, and one that was used over a long period, occurring, as does the straight-sided rectangular (No. 102), with plain and air-twist stems, as well as with white spirals. *Bowls: Other Shapes.*

No genuine piece with the white spiral, that I have ever seen, showed the pontil mark under the foot polished off, though some forgeries do; and with the exception of No. 91, and another piece in Mrs. Rees Price's cabinet, none have the folded foot. The rough pontil mark under the foot may be taken as generic in the case of white and coloured twists. *Feet with Pontil Marks.*

Coloured twists were the natural outcome of a desire for even more variety than could be achieved by the multiplicity and increased *Group IV a: Coloured Twists.*

53

ENGLISH TABLE GLASS

intricacy of white spirals, but are comparatively rare in English pieces. They were perhaps more made at Bristol than elsewhere, and those with a blue twist in the centre of the white (No. 103), or circling round the white centre (No. 104), almost certainly come from that city; while the yellow and white (No. 102) is also probably of the same *fabrique*. No. 101 is red and white—something will be said later as to English spirals of this kind, as contrasted with those of the Low Countries; Mr. Singer's cabinet contains a specimen in which a twist very like No. 99 occurs in pale lavender; and No. 105 is a very handsome specimen showing twists of green, red, and white. Apart from the beauty of their spirals, which make delicious notes of colour when placed among their simpler congeners, they call for little comment.

A word may be said here as to the coloured glasses of this epoch. They seem **Coloured** to be very rare; Mr. Hartshorne **Glasses.** records half a dozen in sapphire blue (drawn and double ogee), which vary in no other detail from the types made in clear white glass; and Mrs. Rees Price has one of later date with a gilt inscription. They all probably partook of the nature of

PLATE XXIV

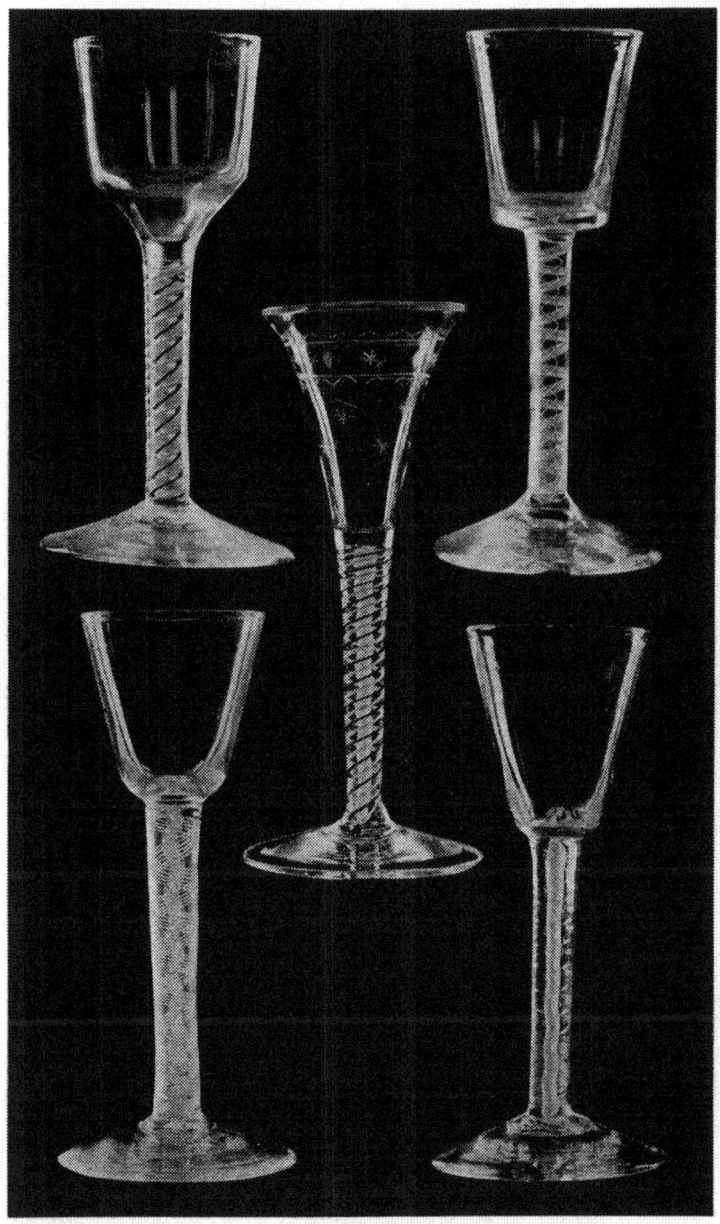

WINE GLASSES. GROUP IVA. COLOURED TWIST STEMS.
101. Height, 6⅛ inches. 105. Height, 6½ inches. 102. Height, 6 inches.
103. Height, 6⅜ inches. 104. Height, 6⅛ inches.

PLATE XXV

WINE GLASSES. GROUP V CUT STEMS.
106. Height, 5⅞ inches. 108. Height, 6⅛ inches. 107. Height, 5⅞ inches.
109. Height, 6 inches. 110. Height, 6⅛ inches.

WINE GLASSES

freaks, and, while doubtless interesting, do not form a link in the series.

Later than these, early in the nineteenth century, we find the funnel-shaped examples (with and without cut flutes), which were made in apple green, and also in an atrocious yellow green, and which were apparently the precursors of the still more or less fashionable coloured bowls stuck on clear stems.

About the fifth group of our eighteenth-century glasses, I have not so much to say; and the illustrations speak for themselves. I am a little inclined to think that cutting was employed on other, and generally larger, objects—bowls, jugs, and standing pieces, as well as salt-cellars—for a good while before it was used on wine glasses; and though we should expect to find the stems of simplest pattern on the earliest specimens of this class, I rather fancy that this is not always the case. The stem of No. 106, for instance, is much more elaborately cut than that of No. 107, while it is pretty clear, from the shape of the bowl and the style of the engraving of the pattern on it, that No. 106 is by a good deal the earlier piece.

Group V: Cut Stems.

The earliest date occurring on a cut-stem

ENGLISH TABLE GLASS

glass seems to be A.D. 1758, and assuming this to be the actual date of the specimen, it would appear to be among the very first of the series. Possibly No. 106 is not much later, but I expect that the majority of these pieces date between A.D. 1775 and A.D. 1800; the latest of all, those in which the foot is cut, as well as bowl and stem, and is thus given the form of a cinquefoil (Nos. 5 and 108), belonging to quite the last years of the century.

By this time our English makers were producing glass of the very finest quality, **The Metal and the Engraving.** hard, clear, pure, and lustrous, and the use of the wheel had come to great perfection. The result is, as might be expected, that we find on the bowls of this series some very good examples of the cutter's and polisher's art —almost like intaglios in their treatment— ranging from the basket of flowers, the grapevine pattern (No. 111), the hop and barley (No. 127), and the queer landscape and figure subjects of quasi-Chinese design (No. 115), to such unusual pieces as No. 218, with the medallion of Britannia. With this use of the polishing wheel, as might be anticipated, the removal of the pontil mark became not

PLATE XXVI

WINE GLASSES. GROUP V. CUT STEMS.
111. Height, 5½ inches. 113. Height, 5 inches. 112. Height, 5⅝ inches.
114. Height, 6 inches. 115. Height, 6⅛ inches.

WINE GLASSES

uncommon; and while some of the pieces figured still retain that odd excrescence, in others it has been polished quite away.

With these wine glasses, in some ways the climax of their makers' art and skill, our long series closes, and we take leave of the eighteenth century. *End of the Series.* Whether the poor taste of the Regent and the Regency, which acted so injuriously on so many of the artistic crafts of our land, was the cause of the subsequent decadence, I know not; it is sufficient to observe that the pieces which succeeded to those we have been considering in the last three chapters lack the beauty and interest of the earlier series, and both because of the limits of the scope of this handbook, and because of their own want of character, they do not call for attention here.

THE SEVENTH CHAPTER
ALE GLASSES AND OTHER TALL PIECES

IN Plates XXVII to XXX we find another set of glasses, analogous, so far as stem types are concerned, to the lengthy series of wine glasses that have just been considered, but lacking the great variety of bowl forms to be found in the smaller pieces. Some of these were ale glasses, and others were doubtless used for light wines; and in the case of those which were not clearly allocated to the less costly brew by the engraving of the familiar hop and barley on the bowls, some doubt as to the actual class to which they belong is inevitable: probably they were used for either beverage indifferently.

However, there can be little hesitation in setting down No. 116 as a wine glass, *A Seventeenth-* though, so far as design is con-
Century cerned, it is fitly associated with
Example. the following pieces. This is an undoubted example of the English glass of the seventeenth century, and at the time that

PLATE XXVII

ALE GLASSES, ETC. BALUSTER STEMS.
116. Height, 7¾ inches.
117. Height, 7⅜ inches. **118.** Height, 7⅜ inches.

ALE GLASSES

it was made it is a little unlikely that ale would be drunk from anything but the metal tankard or the leather jack. But whether it was intended for ale or wine matters little; it is the forerunner, so far as type and design, of the series of tall pieces which now come up for consideration.

Earliest of these, belonging to quite the opening years of the eighteenth century, where it takes its place with such pieces of the baluster-stem type as No. 10, is the second piece figured on Plate XXVII (No. 117); and this piece, too, is just as likely to have been intended for wine as for ale; but the third example (No. 118) tells its own tale, bearing on its bowl the hop and barley to denote the honest home-brewed tipple to the use of which it was dedicated. Chronologically, this, too, comes pretty early in the century, and its companion piece is figured as No. 27. A little later comes No. 119, also showing the hop and barley, and exhibiting with its plain stem a clear affinity to Nos. 2 and 24; and with this we leave the specimens which possess the folded foot.

A glass in the possession of a Brighton collector, with a plain stem of the type of

Baluster Stems and Plain Stems.

ENGLISH TABLE GLASS

No. 28, and a tall bowl of the double ogee form, may have been used for wine, and No. 120, with its handsome bell bowl, may have been designed for champagne; while such tall examples as Nos. 86 and 96 may have served a similar purpose; though I confess to being a little disinclined to bring forward any particular type of eighteenth-century glass as having been exclusively devoted to any individual wine. I am rather of opinion that with our ancestors the wine was the thing, and the glasses counted for little; and if we allow that the specimens with small bowls would naturally be used for the sweeter and heavier vintages, and those with large and tall ones for the lighter wines, we are probably as near as we shall get to the actual facts.

With the tall glasses belonging to the third and fourth stem groups we come to **Air Twists and White Twists.** a few very fine pieces, such a specimen as No. 121, with its richly decorated bowl and handsome knopped stem, being of the very highest quality, both as to metal and design. To this succeed such air-twist pieces as No. 122, closely allied to the single ogee wine glasses, and No. 123, the affinity of which to the straight-sided

PLATE XXVIII

ALE GLASSES, Etc.   PLAIN AND AIR TWIST STEMS.
120. Height, 8¼ inches.
119. Height, 7⅜ inches.   121. Height, 7⅞ inches.

PLATE XXIX

ALE GLASSES, ETC.
AIR TWIST AND WHITE TWIST STEMS.
123. Height, 7⅛ inches.
122. Height, 7½ inches.   124. Height, 7 inches.

ALE GLASSES

ones is clear; and then we pass on to the white twists, Nos. 124 and 125 and 126, of which nothing need be said now, though the distinctly unusual method of decoration of No. 125, the hop and barley being painted in a very thin enamel, will call for comment in a later chapter.

Last of this series comes the splendid piece figured as No. 127, a Bath find of my own, the companion to which was purchased in Bristol by Mrs. Rees Price. Their metal is of a clear pellucid brilliancy, without any trace of the faintly blue tinge sometimes to be found in the glasses with plain stems; and they exhibit the culmination of the powers of the glass cutter and polisher. They are not common, for by this time the tumbler was superseding the tall ale glass, and they are interesting because in them the long sequence draws to its close with a legitimate climax, a *tour de force* of metal and of workmanship.

Cut Stems.

In the first half of the nineteenth century they were succeeded by glasses of the funnel-shaped type, exemplified in the tiny dram glass figured as No. 231, with long cut flutes down the side; and I have a specimen which is inscribed "DISHER'S ALE," Disher

ENGLISH TABLE GLASS

being, I believe, an Edinburgh brewer who was responsible for a special "ten-guinea" ale, which was said to be the strongest ever brewed. But this takes me beyond the definite bounds of my work.

Along with this series of tall-stemmed ale glasses are to be found shorter pieces, in **Smaller Ale Glasses and Goblets.** shape like Nos. 109 and 249, mostly plain stemmed, and almost always engraved with the hop and barley. They lack distinction, and I have not thought it worth while to illustrate them, for every collector will drop across them at the beginning of his enterprise, and will readily recognize them for what they are.

Next to these come the rare short-stemmed goblets, also bearing the familiar hop and barley, and, still smaller and rarer, the specimens which exactly resemble wine glasses, except that they are engraved with the same design as the last. These go back to the white twist period, at any rate, possibly earlier; and were used for the strong old ale which was drawn from the cask and brought to table in special decanters like wine, to be but sparingly partaken of.

Last of all the glasses employed in the consumption of ale or beer come the half-yards

PLATE XXX

ALE GLASSES, ETC.   AIR TWIST AND CUT STEMS.
127. Height, 7⅜ inches.
125. Height, 7¾ inches.   126. Height, 7⅞ inches.

ALE GLASSES

and yards, vessels of varying size and capacity. The earliest mention of the latter seems to be in "Evelyn's Diary," under the year 1685, where the diarist recounts how King James II was proclaimed at Bromley in Kent, His Majesty's health "being drunk in a flint glasse of a yard long." Half-yards, or glasses approximating to that height, which resemble elongated variations of No. 95, with a plain stem, may sometimes be found; and a few glasses which can claim to be a yard long have survived the revelries of a century. These latter are of two forms— those with feet, and those without; the illustrated imperfect specimen (No. 145) from my own cabinet belonging to the former class.

Yards of Ale, etc.

Those without feet generally have a bulb at the base, otherwise resembling the one figured, and this bulb is supposed to render the emptying of them at one draught very difficult, the ale leaving the bulb with a rush and drenching the drinker. But, so far as I know, the difficulty is more imaginary than real; at any rate, I have not found it at all impossible to empty with decorum the only one I ever had in my possession! Being used as tests of skill at merry-makings and convivial assemblies, in which horse-play was

ENGLISH TABLE GLASS

not an unknown factor, most of the many that must have existed have been destroyed, and they are now distinctly rare.

Let me conclude with a warning. Should the collector find a yard glass engraved "*A yard of ale is a dish for a king,*" let him not purchase it as antique; it will be one of half a dozen made a few years ago to the order of an old friend of mine, who, being not unconnected with the brewing of good beer, wished to make a few presents to friends, and selected this distinctly unconventional form.

PLATE XXXI

GOBLET. BALUSTER STEM.
128. Height, 9¾ inches.

Plate XXXII

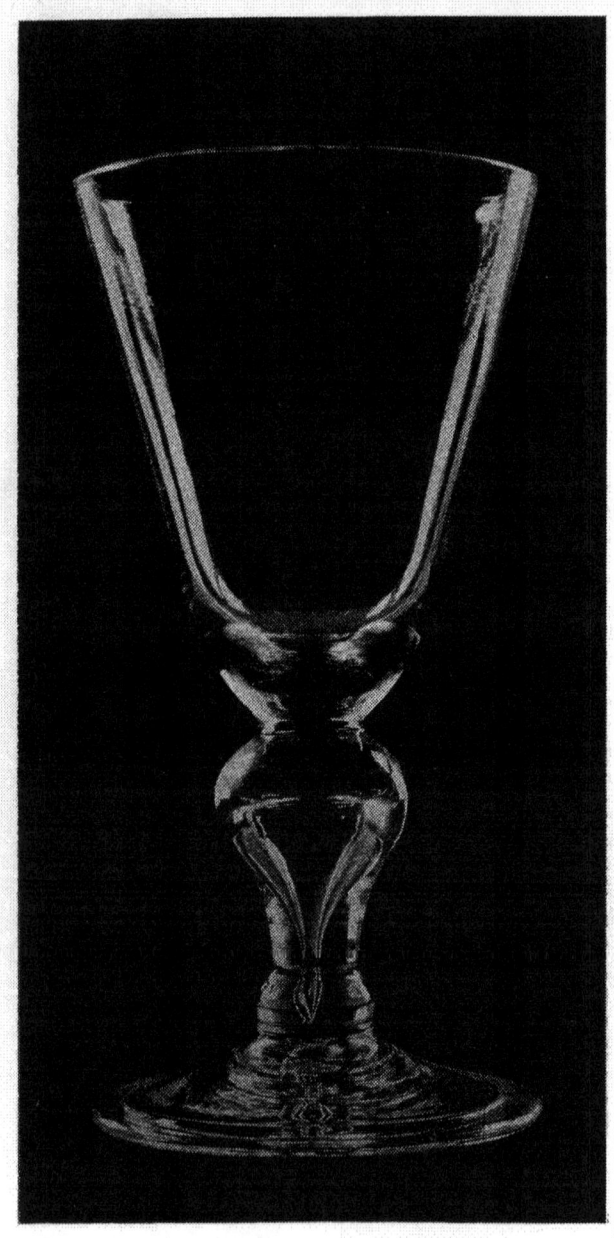

GOBLET. BALUSTER STEM.
129. Height, $9\frac{1}{4}$ inches.

THE EIGHTH CHAPTER
GOBLETS, RUMMERS, CIDER, DRAM, AND SPIRIT GLASSES

ARALLEL to the two series to which attention has already been given, the wine glasses and the tall ale glasses, there runs a series, or rather two, of goblets. The first group consists of gigantic vessels containing any quantity from a quart up to three, and standing from ten to sixteen inches high—huge glasses which, if made for use at all, one would suppose could only have served for ceremonial purposes. The earlier pieces in my own collection, such as Nos. 128, 129, and 130, which approximate to ten inches in height, if used by a single person would certainly afford an abounding draught; on the other hand, they may possibly have served for loving-cups, though one associates this name with tall cups of silver rather than with vessels of glass: the later ones, in which the stem is quite short, and the capacity of the bowl even greater, might possibly have been used as punch-bowls.

Glasses of Heroic Size.

ENGLISH TABLE GLASS

Whatever their purpose, the sequence commences quite early in the century. No. 129 may even be earlier than A.D. 1700; No. 128 is not much later (the date of 1834 and the initials "*R.A.O.*" which this piece bears were added at least a century after it was made); and No. 130, though it does not possess the folded foot of the other two, is probably not much later than A.D. 1750. I have associated this piece with a tiny dram glass of the same shape, as affording rather an amusing contrast and comparison. I also possess later examples, with ogee bowls, one showing an air-twist stem (Group III A), and the other a white spiral; but it was not necessary to illustrate these; they correspond, except for size, to the wine glasses of the same groups.

Another, of a still later date, holding about a pint and a half, and somewhat like No. 139 in form, was given to me by a very kind old friend, as having been made to the order of a bibulous gentleman of old, who used it to keep within the letter of his physician's instructions, when the medical man ordered him to drink only one glass of port at dinner!

These huge glasses are not very common, and the collector need not fear that his available space will be curtailed if he acquires

PLATE XXXIII

GOBLET.
DRAWN STEM
130. Height, 9½ inches

LIQUEUR GLASS.
DRAWN STEM.
131. Height, 3½ inches.

PLATE XXXIV

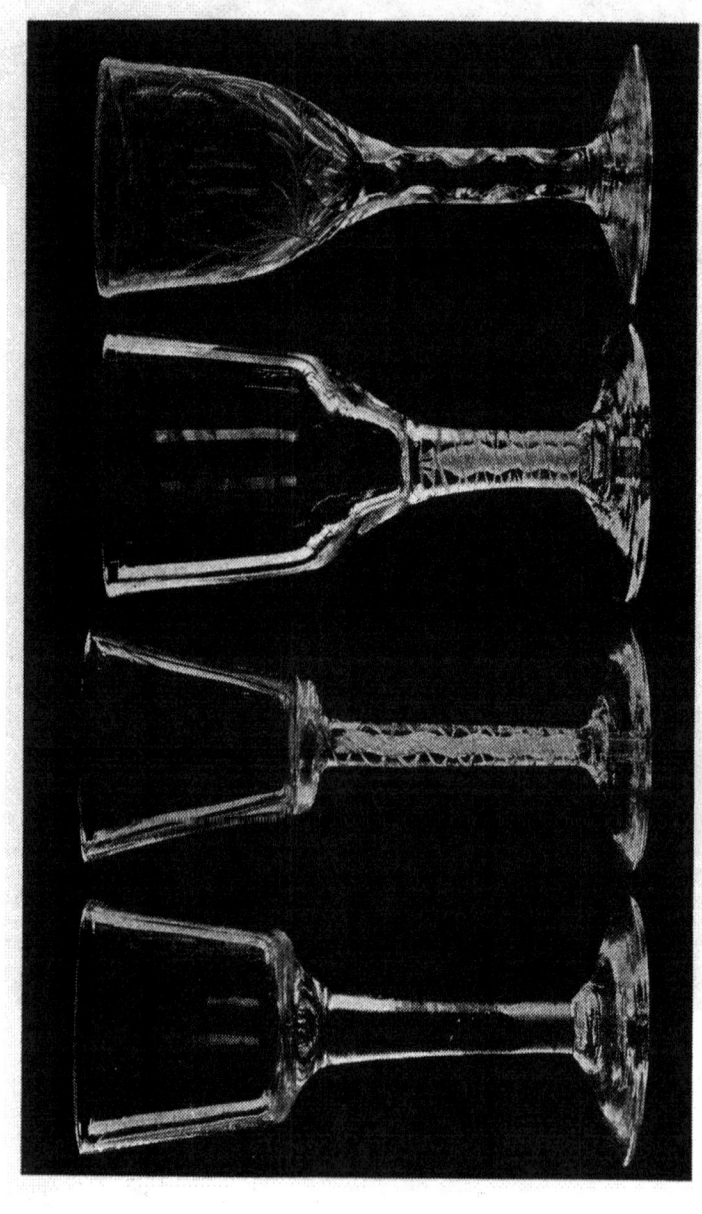

RUMMERS. FOUR TYPES OF STEM.

132. Plain Stem. Height, 6⅞ inches. 133. Air Twist Stem. Height, 6⅞ inches. 134. White Twist Stem. Height, 6⅝ inches. 135. Cut Stem. Height, 6⅞ inches.

GOBLETS AND RUMMERS

them when he can. The possession of a few is desirable; their very size and bulk is impressive, they form admirable centres round which the smaller contemporary glasses may cluster, and their Herculean capacity leads the memory back with a smile to the days when an Englishman's draught, like that of the Dutchman famous in song, was "as deep as the rolling Zuyder Zee"!

Plate XXXIV is devoted to the illustration of specimens of the second group of goblets or rummers, those of normal size, which show that the usual stem sequence is to be found in this series as well as in the wine glasses and ale glasses. In my own cabinet there is also a piece of similar capacity of the baluster-stem period, but it was not necessary to reproduce this; nor is it necessary to say much more about these rummers and those illustrated in the next two plates, though one or two details call for note. *Rummers of Four Types.*

It has been already pointed out that it is quite probable that the tall glasses described in the last chapter were used indiscriminately for wine or strong ale; and it is quite likely that these rummers were used for other liquors as well as for *Cider Glasses.*

ENGLISH TABLE GLASS

grog or toddy—cider, for instance, or the less common perry. But whether the straight-sided rectangular pieces (No. 133, for example) were wholly and solely cider glasses, as has been suggested—made for the first time in A.D. 1763 in support of the popular protest against a duty on this home-made beverage—is to me very doubtful. Any glass which bears engraved on the bowl an apple-tree, or a border of apples and leaves, or a motto distinctly allusive to cider, may be fairly assigned to that favourite west-country tipple, which was so strong that it was taken in small glasses like wine (*e.g.* Nos. 225 and 226); and it is a fact that one or two pieces so inscribed and decorated do belong to this straight-sided rectangular type. But I think this is most likely due to the fact that *circa* A.D. 1760 this was a fashionable shape (in Mr. Singer's collection are two bearing that date), so that it was really almost inevitable that on some glasses of this form should be recorded the farmer's protest against the obnoxious excise duties on cider and other liquors which roused him to revolt in A.D. 1763.

En passant the two-handled cup (No. 136), apparently based as to form on contemporary

PLATE XXXV

RUMMER.　　　　TWO-HANDLED CUP.　　　　RUMMER.
137. Height, 4⅞ inches.　　136. Height, 6¼ inches.　　138. Height, 5⅜ inches.

PLATE XXXVI

RUMMERS, ETC.
139. Height, 5 inches. 140. Height, 6¼ inches. 141. Height, 4¾ inches.

MUGS AND TUMBLERS

silver pieces, calls for a little attention, as being unusual; and the quaint piece figured as No. 140, which is of later date, was possibly made at Glasgow, and if so, is one of the comparatively few specimens definitely known to proceed from some individual glass-house. The square-footed type (No. 138), with bowls of varying fashions, belongs to about A.D. 1775-80; and the mugs and tankards illustrated come quite at the end of the series and the century, in some cases doubtless passing beyond A.D. 1800. *Later Pieces: Mugs and Tumblers.*

With these I close the series of the larger vessels, illustrating few tumblers (Nos. 220, 221, and 243), chiefly because, though they are a long series and occur all through the century, they naturally present no variations in form, except that sometimes they assume the barrel shape. The date of any specimen may be approximately determined from the style of its decoration; the two illustrated in Plate LVIII belong to within a year or two of A.D. 1780.

The rather insignificant little glasses figured in Plates XXXVIII, XXXIX, and XL are some of those which were devoted to aqua vitæ, strong *Dram and Spirit Glasses.*

69

ENGLISH TABLE GLASS

waters, cordials, and liqueurs. As the saying is to-day in Scotland, they hold a "dram." If I had chosen to illustrate the whole series, it would have been possible to make clear in these short and dumpy little vessels the same sequence of stems, if not of bowls, as has already been established among the larger glasses; but I thought this unnecessary, and have simply chosen for illustration a few varying types of the plainer makes. Doubtless some of the taller pieces of small capacity were used for liqueurs (Nos. 42 and 74 are illustrations of this, and I possess another example from Braintree which closely resembles No. 3, but only holds a very small quantity); but the height and general appearance of these glasses naturally leads to their inclusion, as they have been placed here, among wine glasses, where, after all, they are more fully displayed.

A curious little set of these glasses, obviously holding the most trifling quan-
Friends to Temperance. tities of spirit, is reproduced in Plate XXXVIII. No. 146 comes quite early in the eighteenth century, No. 147 probably belongs to the early years of the nineteenth, and the other two are intermediate. No. 147 was given to me by my

MUGS OR TANKARDS.

142. Height, 5½ inches.   143. Height, 5⅛ inches.   144. Height, 5⅝ inches.

PLATE XXXVIII

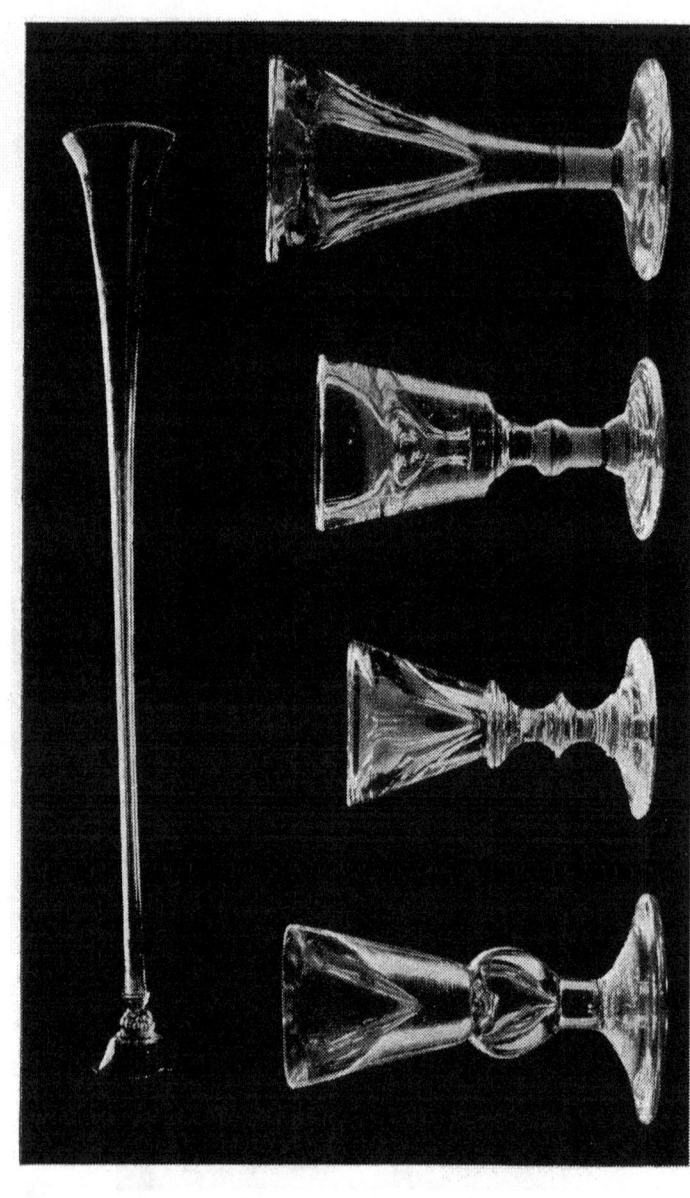

145. YARD-OF-ALE GLASS. Length of original, 33 inches.
DRAWN GLASSES.
146. Height, 4¾ inches.   147. Height, 3⅝ inches.   148. Height, 4⅛ inches.   149. Height, 4⅞ inches

SPIRIT GLASSES

friend Mr. John Lane, who got it as a "Joey" glass from the Queen's Head at Box, near Bath, which was an old coaching-house. "Joeys" were fourpenny pieces, so called after Mr. Joseph Hume, M.P., at whose instance they were coined; and these glasses were provided for the refreshment of the travellers on passing coaches, as holding four pennyworth of brandy. When filled, they present a normal appearance, the thick, heavy sides vanishing; when emptied, the fraud is apparent both to eye and palate! Nos. 148 and 149 came from Carlisle, another great coaching focus; and the good lady who sold them to me knew all about their deceptive aspect when full, and as we talked of it she chuckled her joy (with the broadest Cumberland burr) at "the waay we used to fool the poor Scoatch fowk!"

There is another uncommon type of glasses associated with the old coaching days, and though they quite possibly belong to the nineteenth century, they may be mentioned here. They are funnel-shaped glasses from four to six inches high, cut in flutes after the style of No. 231, but in place of the usual foot they have simply a small knob, so that they can

Other Travellers' Glasses.

ENGLISH TABLE GLASS

only stand upside down. On the coach arriving at an inn for a change of horses, a tray full of these would be brought out, the passengers would seize one each, which would be filled from the various decanters by the servant, they were emptied without delay, and the coach would roll on. These glasses are not of frequent occurrence, Mr. Hartshorne records some, and there are specimens in Mr. Singer's collection; but I have never found one myself.

Nos. 151 and 152 are Scotch pieces, the former, like some other "firing" glasses here figured (*cf.* Nos. 158 and 162), having a thick and massive base with which to knock on the table when applause was to be given to song, sentiment, or toast; and the charming little "thistle" glass, figured as No. 164, is also Scotch, and I have thought it well to include it as a genuine example of a freely imitated type, even though it possibly does not belong quite to the eighteenth century. The double glass, reproduced as No. 159, is curious; the ogee piece (No. 162) is interesting as being almost a facsimile of Benjamin Franklin's glass, now belonging to the Historical Society of Pennsylvania; the little barrels, Nos. 160 and 161 (with their congener,

Plate XXXIX

DRAM AND SPIRIT GLASSES.

150. Height, 4¾ inches. 151. Height, 3¾ inches. 152. Height, 4⅝ inches.
154. Height, 3⅞ inches. 153. Height, 1⅞ inches. 156. Height, 4½ inches.
155. Height, 4¼ inches.

Plate XL

DRAM AND SPIRIT GLASSES.

157. Height, 4⅝ inches. 158. Height, 3¾ inches 159. Height, 4¼ inches.
160. Height, 1¾ inches. 164. Height, 4⅝ inches 161. Height, 1⅝ inches.
162. Height, 4¾ inches.   163. Height, 4⅞ inches.

SPIRIT GLASSES

No. 153), are quite quaint, though they come late; and lastly, No. 154 has been illustrated, though with No. 156 it belongs *circa* A.D. 1820, because it shows the amazing persistency of a simple piece of decoration, that rough and highly conventional " rose " which may be observed (see Nos. 26 and 27) at least a hundred years earlier.

THE NINTH CHAPTER
CANDLESTICKS, DECANTERS, SWEETMEAT GLASSES, TRAILED PIECES, ETC.

ARALLEL to the long sequence of drinking glasses just described there run two other series of table utensils which were quite as much decorative as utilitarian, the sweetmeat glasses (of which more presently) and the candlesticks. Good taste, **Candlesticks: also a Series.** or perhaps I should say fastidious taste, demands that complete harmony should pervade the furnishing and appurtenances of a table; and so we find that of these latter quaint and graceful objects it is quite possible to collect a sequence as interesting as that of the concurrent wine glasses, and showing, for the most part, the same decorative characteristics and methods, the same typical stems, feet, and pontil marks. Early come big lumpy pieces (one massive example in my own possession, with the characteristic folded foot, and standing 8½ inches high, has a base no less than 6½ inches in diameter), and these are followed by such pretty examples as No. 165

PLATE XLI

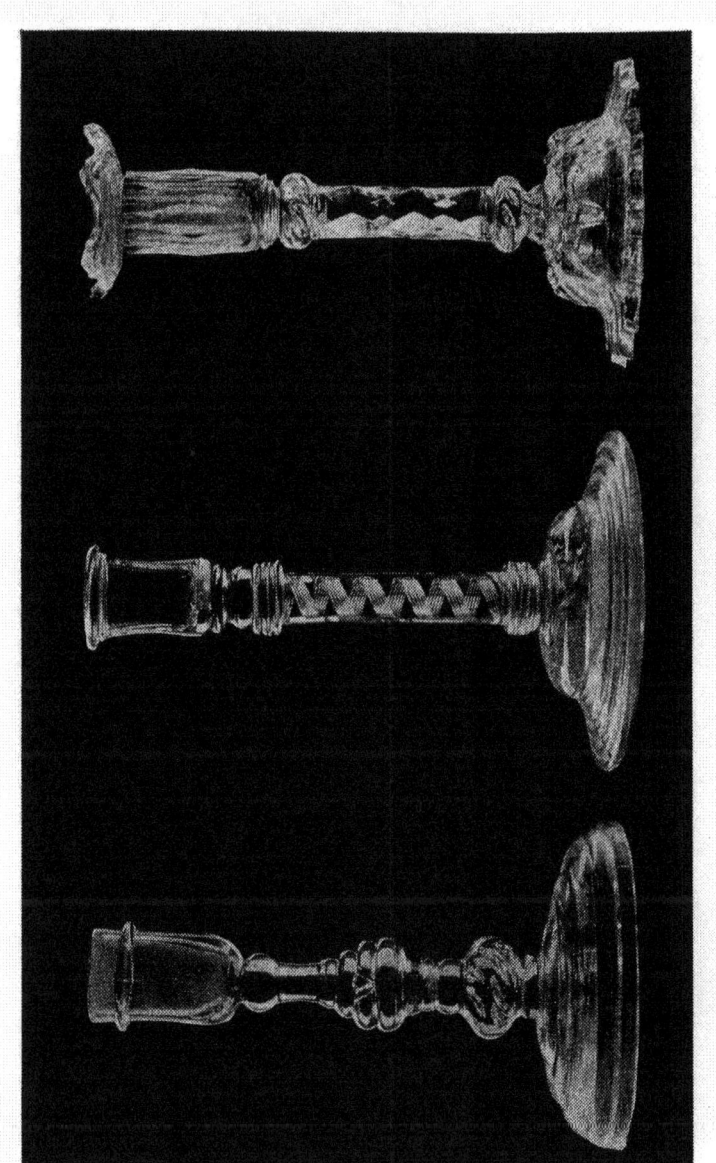

CANDLESTICKS.

165. Height, 6¾ inches.   166. Height, 6¾ inches.   167. Height, 6⅞ inches.

PLATE XLII

TODDY FILLER.   DECANTER.   TODDY FILLER.
168. Height, 7⅜ inches.   170. Height, 11½ inches.   169. Height, 7¼ inches.

BOTTLES AND DECANTERS

(consorting with plain stem glasses); No. 166, with its air twist; and No. 167, showing a well-cut stem and nozzle; while the intermediate white screw, though not illustrated here, is not uncommon.

For the most part, the decanters which belong to the eighteenth century lack the beauty and the interest attaching to the wine and other glasses; they do not extend over so long a period, nor do they exhibit the variety of form and decoration which, as we have seen, mark the drinking vessels. During the greater part of the eighteenth century wine was probably brought to the table in the well-known big-bellied black bottle, with its impressed seal; and when, later, decanters of clear glass came into fashion, they were quite unassuming and simple in form. Plate XLII shows a fine example, of fairly early date, in my own cabinet, and Mrs. Rees Price has two similar pieces, each holding more than half a gallon. The date of these can be gauged fairly accurately from the characteristic festoons with which they are adorned. At a little later date decanters became more globular, sometimes having serrated ridges passing from base to top; at others bearing initials

ENGLISH TABLE GLASS

and emblems, as in the case of the one in my collection which has the initials *T. M. B.* on one side, and on the other the shuttle and shears, which indicate that it once belonged to a weaver who was proud of his trade.

Still later, about the end of the century, the type exemplified by the two examples figured in Plate XLIII came into vogue; the one (No. 171) inscribed "THE LAND WE LIVE IN," and showing perpendicular corrugations akin to those on such glasses as No. 93, being perhaps a little earlier than No. 172, which (according to the inscription on it) was "USED AT THE CORONATION OF GEORGE THE IV. IN WESTMINSTER HALL 19 JULY, 1821." With this, and with the heavy and cumbrous cut specimens so frequently met with, we pass beyond the century.

The two curious objects, Nos. 168 and 169, figured on Plate XLII, are also (judging from the character of the cutting) probably of the early years of the nineteenth century; but they are included because they are not well known south of the Tweed, and because it is not impossible that earlier specimens may be found. They were used in place of the familiar ladle of the eighteenth century to fill glasses from the punch-

Toddy Fillers.

PLATE XLIII

DECANTERS, Etc.
171. Height, 6½ inches.   172. Height, 6¼ inches.
173. Height, 6⅜ inches.

PLATE XLIV

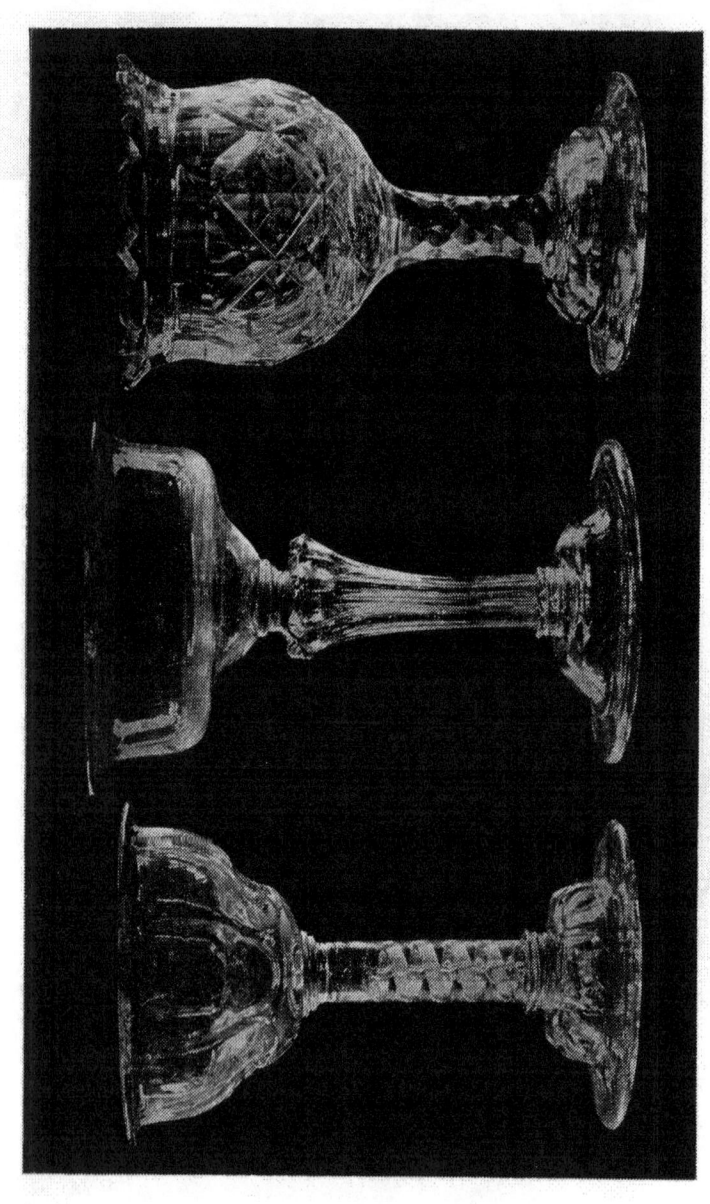

SWEETMEAT GLASSES.
174. Height, 6¼ inches. 175. Height, 6⅞ inches. 176. Height, 6⅜ inches.

SWEETMEAT GLASSES

or toddy-bowl—being inserted in the bowl until the bulb (which holds a glassful) was filled through the hole in its base, they could then be lifted with the thumb held at the top of the tube, and the toddy transferred to the glass simply by removing the thumb.

With the handsome and finely designed pieces figured as Nos. 173 to 180, in which may be traced the same sequence (and the same characteristics as to feet and pontil marks) as have been noted in the wine glasses and candlesticks, I come to a group of vessels which personally I find a little perplexing. Such specimens as Nos. 174, 175, 177, and 178 are classed by Mr. Hartshorne as early champagne glasses; while those which have a purfled or frilled edge to the lip (I regret that I cannot illustrate the excellent example in Mr. Singer's cabinet), and those which show a cut and vandyked edge (Nos. 176 and 179) he calls sweetmeat glasses. This division may be quite correct; but if the earlier specimens of the obviously long and complete series were drinking glasses (*e.g.* Nos. 174 and 175), why do we *never* find examples of the cut-stem type which it would be possible to use to drink from?

Sweetmeat Glasses, etc.

ENGLISH TABLE GLASS

Let us, for example, consider those two pieces, Nos. 177 and 179 (Plate XLV), clearly one of the earliest and one of the latest of the sequence. From No. 177 it is possible, though not comfortable, to drink; in the case of No. 179 it is obviously out of the question. And my feeling is that neither were intended for drinking vessels, for the difference existing between these two specimens are solely those of fashion; the one has descended from the other, *mutatis mutandis* they are the same thing, the analogy between them as to form and design is complete, and to me the deduction that they were made for one purpose seems to be not only justified but inevitable—in short, that they were all sweetmeat glasses.

But whether they were champagne glasses, or whether they were used for sweetmeats, they are handsome objects, with their almost constant domed feet—sometimes ridged or corrugated, sometimes plain, sometimes cut —their handsome stems and graceful bowls; and one of the very finest I have ever seen is that figured as No. 180. This piece has one fault—its foot is rather too small; otherwise we cannot praise too highly the graceful dome of the foot, the well-made "collars" at the

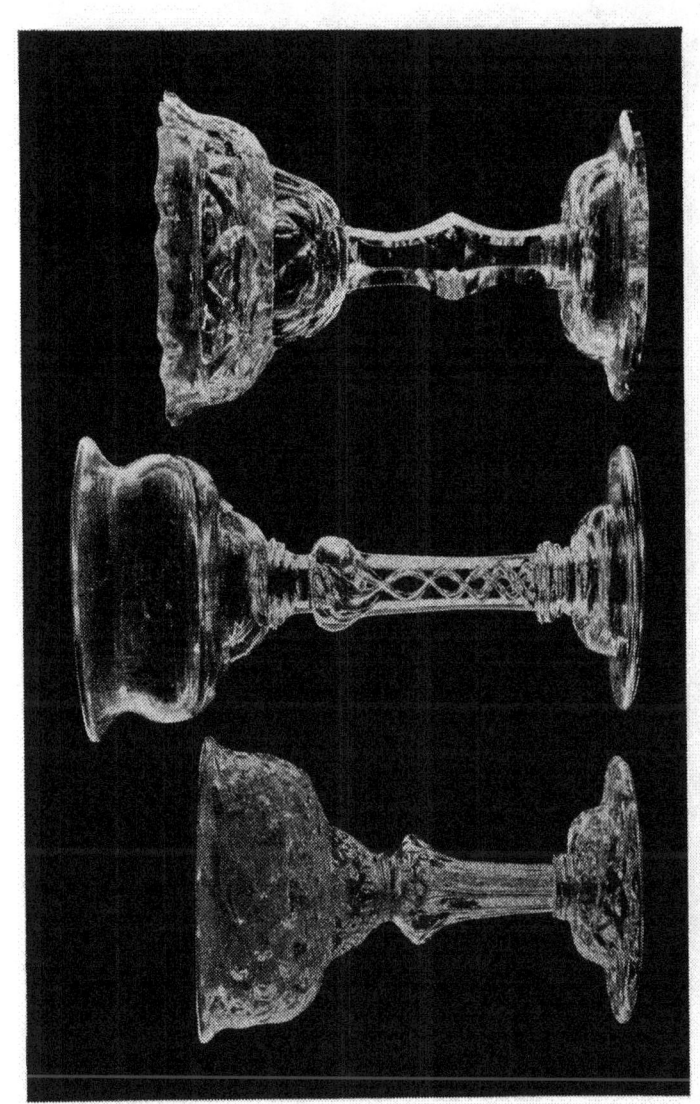

SWEETMEAT GLASSES.

177. Height, 5⅜ inches. **178.** Height, 7⅛ inches. **179.** Height, 6 inches.

PLATE XLVI

SWEETMEAT
GLASS.

180. Height, 7½ inches.

BELL, WITH
TRAILED DECORATION.

181. Height, 7⅞ inches.

BOWLS AND PORRINGERS

top and bottom of the stem, the twist consisting of a double blue thread that runs outside the white network in the stem, the fine sweep of the double ogee bowl, and the characteristically simple and effective network engraving. If the blue-twist wine glasses may be assigned to Bristol, this follows; but wherever it was made it was the work of a master of his craft and its possibilities.

The last group of glass vessels to be noticed in these pages comprises some massive and stately pieces, bowls, porringers, covered cups, etc., which possess the common characteristic of being decorated in zigzag patterns with ridges or raised trails of glass. Typical examples are figured on Plates XLVI, XLVII, and XLVIII, and in these the various patterns of trailing are pretty completely exemplified. *Pieces with Trailed Decoration.*

Vessels of glass, as a rule, do not simulate the forms peculiar to those in other materials, though occasionally one finds a candlestick clearly copied from a metal one, or a cup (see No. 136) the design of which is based on an example in silver. But though I doubt if my two-handled porringer (Plate XLVIII) was made for use, or was intended

ENGLISH TABLE GLASS

for any purpose beyond being displayed on a sideboard, it is interesting as being obviously based on the similar silver pieces of the seventeenth and early eighteenth centuries; while to me it possesses the additional interest of bearing the mark of the original owner, some glass lover of a century and a half ago, at least, whose initials —whatever his name was—were the same as my own: a little coincidence that seems somehow to bridge the years, to link the present to a bygone age.

Some of these pieces have deeply folded feet; others, like those figured, have feet irregularly scolloped; some have a very rough pontil mark; the metal of many is deep in tone and heavy; and all, I fancy, belong to the earlier forty years of the eighteenth century. The bell could have been used, and so could the jugs; the bowls might be punch-bowls, and the covered cups might also serve some useful purpose; but all the same, my conclusion is that they were "parade pieces," meant for display, were intended to gleam on the sideboard rather than to serve any utilitarian purpose on the table.

PLATE XLVII

COVERED BOWL, WITH TRAILED DECORATION.
182. Height, 7⅞ inches.

Plate XLVIII

PORRINGER. WITH TRAILED DECORATION.
183. Height, 11½ inches.

THE TENTH CHAPTER
METHODS OF DECORATION

ROM the numerous examples of decorated bowls to be found among the examples reproduced in the plates, it is obvious that more methods than one were employed to give added richness to the appearance of the glasses. Of the different flutings, grooves, and ribbings, examples have been illustrated, and need not be repeated; but it has been thought well to bring together in one illustration, for purposes of comparison, specimens of the other fashions of bowl decoration.

Naturally engraving on the wheel was one of the earliest methods employed, and No. 187 exemplifies the effect, at once rich and simple, that could easily be obtained by it, and shows the frequent conventional vine pattern in one of its many forms. (No. 184 shows the same method employed to render a rarer version of the same motive, the growing vine.) Later, as in No. 186, came the fashion of polishing part of the engraving to add lightness to the

Varieties of Engraving.

ENGLISH TABLE GLASS

effect; and this was succeeded, quite towards the end of the century, by the entirely polished engraving so well seen in No. 189.

Some of the Patterns. The patterns themselves are not very numerous, but they show many variations, and some are curiously persistent. The vine has many forms, so has the rose, the latter ranging from the simple convention seen in No. 26 to the elaborate and naturalistic effects found in Nos. 31 and 202. On other wine-glasses of different dates are to be found the sunflower, lily of the valley, forget-me-not, tulip, honeysuckle, and rose of Sharon; while the hop and barley are naturally and appropriately placed on ale glasses. Then we also find butterflies, bees, moths, swans, and the curious hovering bird which may be traced from such early examples as No. 22 to quite late pieces like No. 139. Little landscapes, sometimes naturalistic, sometimes pseudo-Chinese in their convention, are also to be found; as are figure subjects, and the sporting scenes, coats-of-arms, ships, inscriptions, badges, and emblems to be spoken of in Chapter XII. These engravings, while usually placed on the bowls, are also to be found in the foot, as in the case of a Jacobite glass in the Singer collection,

PLATE XLIX

METHODS OF DECORATION.

184.   185. Height, 3⅝ inches.   186.
187.   188.   189.
190.   191.   192.

METHODS OF DECORATION

and two which belonged to Admiral Robertson Macdonald, and even under the foot, as in No. 202 in my own cabinet, which bears beneath the base a beautifully engraved heraldic rose and leaves. Whether this position of these emblems has anything to do with the old-time fashion of holding and lifting glasses by the foot (and not by the stem, as we do to-day), I cannot say.

Sometimes these engraved patterns were oil gilt, and a very rich effect was thereby produced; No. 210, for instance, shows a few traces of this, while No. 237, which is practically in its pristine condition, exemplifies this somewhat unusual method still better. Other gilt decorations were burnished, the gold being applied to the surface of the glass without any engraving, and lightly fixed; and of this method Mr. Singer's cabinet contains a fine example, the bowl of a rummer being almost covered with trails of vine; while No. 192, though less important as to size, also exemplifies quite well this fashion of decoration.

Gilding and Enamel.

The white enamelled decoration sometimes found on these glasses is of two kinds. In the first (see No. 190) the designs are painted with considerable "body" and density; in the

ENGLISH TABLE GLASS

other (of which No. 188 is a fine example), the enamel consists of the merest film, most delicately applied, the necessary outlines and veinings being attained by the employment of a needle to remove the film in the manner of an etcher. Both methods are rare, and the latter is the less common—indeed, it seems only to be employed on ale glasses to render the hop and barley pattern; while in the coarser enamel we find the familiar scrolls, festoons, and vine leaves, as well as very quaint and interesting sporting scenes, hunting, shooting, skating, etc. It is possible that these enamelled glasses may have been made in Bristol, where white opaque glass bottles and other vessels were made and decorated in colours.

In many cases where the design on an inscribed glass has been executed on the wheel, the accompanying inscription has been written with the diamond-point (see No. 245); in other examples the whole design has been so engraved. Mrs. Rees Price has a large glass so treated, with a view of a vessel at sea, a cliff, and a fort, freely and sketchily handled; and the elaborate lettering of No. 224, and the coat-of-arms (Arundell?) reproduced rather

Diamond-point Engravings.

METHODS OF DECORATION

more than half size for the sake of clearness, as No. 191 (from a bowl), afford further examples of this particular fashion of decoration. It is a fashion that dates from the earliest times, and is found in all countries; the Elizabethan example figured in Plate II is so decorated, and doubtless earlier examples could be found; while it is not yet, I believe, extinct. Mrs. Rees Price has two late goblets so engraved, covered with military and sporting emblems, coats-of-arms, etc., and I possess one obviously from the same hand, which bears amid a multiplicity of designs a poem by Burns and an inscription stating that it was "presented to Mrs. Rogers by J. Crofts, 2nd Life Guards," as well as the engraver's signature, "*J. Wickenden* 1853."

It is almost an unknown thing for the craftsman to sign his work on decorated English glasses. The names of the executants of these quaint designs have perished, and we can now identify none of the users of the wheel and the diamond-point, except Giles of York, who worked in both styles about A.D. 1756, and Felix Foster, who wielded the diamond-point at the same date. Of these the lineal artistic descendant, however debased his style, was J. Wickenden.

ENGLISH TABLE GLASS

The English glass engravers of the eighteenth century were not, as a rule, artists, **Fluoric Acid Etching.** though many were highly trained craftsmen; but there was one set of workers who devoted themselves to the decoration of glasses who were possessed of true and remarkable artistic talent, as well as of unrivalled deftness and skill in the manipulation of their peculiar process. These were the creators of the delicate designs, etched by means of fluoric acid, upon the bowls of such examples as Nos. 193 and 194. Beautifully drawn, exquisitely faint and clear, resembling nothing so much as a film of mist blown upon the surface of the bowl, they are the most beautiful decorations, I think, ever used on any glasses.

This art, originating probably in Germany, had many practitioners there and in the Low Countries, whose names do not here concern us. It is not at all improbable that it was also employed in this country, though less extensively than in its place of origin; and No. 185, a quaint little glass thus decorated with a landscape, bears every evidence of being English, both in manufacture and ornament. This specimen, by the way, is said to have belonged to George III; and

PLATE L

GLASSES DECORATED BY MEANS OF FLUORIC ACID.
183. Height, 10⅝ inches.   194. Height, 8¼ inches.

METHODS OF DECORATION

there seems to be no reason to doubt the attribution. English names also occur among these workers in fluoric acid. Greenwood, sometimes included among the Dutch artists, is responsible for the fine example figured as No. 193, and Adams (another distinctly English name) was the decorator of a glass I have noted, which bears on its bowl Bacchus and his vine, with the suggestive inscription, "May we never want its fruit."

The custom of marking the black "big-bellied bottles" of the eighteenth century with the date, name, or arms of the owner, impressed on a glass seal stuck on the side of the bottle, is known to all collectors; and Mr. Hartshorne records one wine glass (with a white twist stem) thus decorated on each side of the bowl with an impressed coat-of-arms. It is a very rare example; and with this method of decoration, known so far only by this solitary instance, this chapter fitly closes.

Impressed Seals.

THE ELEVENTH CHAPTER
FRAUDS, FAKES, AND FORGERIES: FOREIGN GLASS

IT is very difficult to convey, by any written description, the difference between a genuine product of antiquity, in any *genre*, and its modern imitation; and in the case of glass it is particularly far from easy. But there are a few general characteristics which may be mentioned for the guidance of collectors, though there is no real equipment for the discrimination of the spurious, save experience and the instinct which comes of the handling of many examples.

The foot of a glass is naturally the first thing that a collector looks at, and a pretty full description of the varieties found in genuine pieces is given in Chapter III. A glass which lacks the pontil mark, purporting to belong to any other group than that with the cut stems, should almost invariably be rejected; though here a certain amount of discrimination must be exercised, because of the existence of certain glasses which may be

Feet and their Characteristics.

Plate LI. FORGERIES. 195. 196. 197. 198.

FRAUDS AND FORGERIES

described as survivals or replacements. Mrs. Rees Price has two specimens with air-twist stems (not drawn), the bowls of which bear the Hanoverian emblem of the white horse, with the motto "LIBERTY" (*cf.* No. 215), and in these pieces the pontil mark has been polished off. But all the same, there is no reason to doubt their authenticity, and they were possibly made very late in the eighteenth century to complete a set by replacing earlier glasses unfortunately broken. Other examples have come under my notice, but this will suffice to illustrate the point.

The form of the foot on genuine pieces is also notable; they are almost always large (the diameter being at least of the bowl) to ensure stability, and when not domed, are generally markedly conical in form. This has been well described as "having a high instep"—the characteristic of a glass of long descent, as well as of a lady of lofty pedigree! Look for a moment at No. 24, and then turn to No. 197; the latter pseudo-Jacobite specimen is the modern forger's product, and exemplifies at once his lack of skill in making an air twist, and his failure to achieve the proper foot—it is flat and thin, and lacks the pontil mark.

ENGLISH TABLE GLASS

It need scarcely be added that when the collector finds a piece, the foot of which never had a pontil mark, he should at once reject it. Those glasses in which the under side of the foot is of waxy smoothness (not polished) are rank impostures, and are not infrequently found of the type of No. 195. Sometimes the bowls of these particular fabrications are gilt; at other times they are enamelled or engraved (this one is dated 1714!), but once seen and identified for what they are, they will always be known.

Any glasses in which the spiral in the stem runs the reverse way to the normal **Stems and Spirals.** may be considered spurious, and so may pieces in which poor blue or red threads are found with no white interspersed, as well as examples in which the red or green threads are supplemented by white twists irregularly and imperfectly formed. These at present seem to be chiefly produced with bell bowls, but other types may be found. In the air twists, as in the white ones, the forger is often unequal to the production of a satisfactory imitation; but in the cut stems he is quite capable of rivalling the work of a century ago, and such pieces as No. 198 are made in large

FRAUDS AND FORGERIES

quantities, and are often sold with intent to deceive. Here the stem does not rise from the base quite correctly, and while the cutting and engraving are excellently imitated from the old pieces, the sides of the bowl are about double the thickness of those in genuine examples.

In the course of the preceding chapters little variations in the metal of different types of glasses have been noted as far as possible, and as far as could be conveyed in written words; but only slight allusion has been made to the "ring" of all good English pieces. If a glass, on being tapped or flicked with the finger-nail, fails to give a clear, true ring, it must be regarded with extreme suspicion—it is probably either spurious or the inferior product of some Low Country glass-house. And if the metal is *too* clear and brilliant, that also gives cause for grave suspicion; but this latter is a matter that can often only be settled by actual comparison with undoubted pieces of the style and reputed date of the dubious example.

A wicked person, whose name I mercifully withhold, once submitted No. 196 to my inspection as a very fine "Williamite" glass, recently sent him. Its form, as will be

Metal and "Ring."

ENGLISH TABLE GLASS

seen, is a little unusual, but scarcely abnormal; it rings beautifully; the engraving is just what one would expect to find; the foot, while scarcely so "high in the instep" as might be anticipated, yet bears the right fold and pontil mark;—and yet for some reason, when I handled it, I was not satisfied. I could not say why; it all *seemed* correct, and, though my instinct made me doubt it, I could not condemn it until I placed it among others. Then the absolute colourless clarity of the glass became apparent, and I told my friend that if he had not already bought it, he would be well advised to return it. Then the unhappy man confessed that it was an absolute copy of a genuine piece, made to his order by a well-known firm of glass-blowers, and further treated by himself in one or two apparently trivial but essential details (not necessary to repeat here), so as to simulate the original absolutely! Luckily for my reputation as a judge of glasses, the appearance of the old metal could not be imitated; but even to a keen eye the copy was so accurate as to deceive in every detail but that.

This is an unusual instance, but I tell the tale to point once more the moral, that in the

PITFALLS AND PROBLEMS

last resort—in glass as in china and pictures —the cultured eye and the connoisseur's instinct are the only safe guides.

There are various other circumstances which may induce doubt in the mind of a collector, and one curious case may be illustrated from No. 128, and from a piece presenting similar features in Mrs. Rees Price's collection. This latter is an air-twist (drawn) glass, dating approximately from A.D. 1755, but bearing an inscription written with a diamond in later years of the nineteenth century; the former, though a glass of about A.D. 1725, is similarly inscribed, "*R.A.O.* 1834." In each case, of course, the inscription has been placed on an early and genuine glass, and might lead to a misapprehension of the true character of the specimen if its characteristics were not well marked; and even more puzzling and troublesome are the instances, of which I know a few, in which eighteenth-century glasses profess to commemorate seventeenth-century historical events.

In these particular cases, the inscriptions have been placed on the bowls without any fraudulent idea. There was some reason for them, apart from any desire to create a

ENGLISH TABLE GLASS

spurious antique; but it is easy to see how simple a matter it would be for the forger or the faker to take a genuine glass and add to it some emblem or design which (if genuine and contemporary) would greatly increase the interest and value of the specimen. This form of deception is one to be most carefully guarded against, and every inscribed glass demands very complete examination before it is accepted.

However, these instances of misleading inscriptions are uncommon, and the more **Foreign Glasses.** frequent problems are presented by those glasses which might equally justly be attributed either to England or to Holland. Some of the Dutch glasses, being produced in the same way as the English ones, and to similar designs, naturally bear a great resemblance to our own, and are really very hard to distinguish from them. Particularly is this the case with some glasses with bell bowls and white twist stems; others are easily differentiated by reason of their weak twists, the poor colour of the threads (the white being bluish, and not dense and true —milk-and-water compared to the milk-white of good pieces), and the lightness of the metal and the almost straw-colour pervading it.

PITFALLS AND PROBLEMS

Summary. In brief, then, a would-be buyer of any glass should study the type and details of the foot, examine the craftsmanship and structure of the stem, consider the colour and density of the twist, test the ring of the bowl and the colour of the metal, and regard with care the niceties of the decoration — engraving, enamelling, or gilding. Should he find an example which puzzles him, though he cannot pronounce it spurious, it does no harm to purchase. A "problem piece" is always interesting and always valuable. If it turns out to be a fraud or a fake, the collector has learnt the lesson it conveys; if it should be a rare or unusual specimen of genuine character, his collection is all the stronger, his judgment the sounder, and his knowledge the wider.

Finally—*Caveat Emptor*.

THE TWELFTH CHAPTER
INSCRIBED AND HISTORIC GLASSES

IN an earlier chapter it has been pointed out that, in addition to the artistic value of the individual specimens, and the antiquarian interest of the several series into which these glasses fall, there clings to many examples a sentiment more intimate and personal, sometimes by reason of the inscriptions or emblems engraved upon them, sometimes on account of the known history of the particular piece in question. To treat at large on these inscribed and historic pieces, which strike a note at once curiously human and strangely familiar—to attempt to formulate for them, as for their less uncommon congeners, a succession and a classification—would demand far more space than is at my disposal, and could not, after all, lead to very much profit. For while, in some cases, the symbols and inscriptions which adorn these glasses have reference to a cult or a creed, which permits of their being grouped together, the charm

INSCRIBED GLASSES

of many lies in their individuality and their entire lack of association with others. Possibly, under these circumstances, the simplest and most useful chapter that can be compiled in this connection, will be one containing some slight account of the examples actually illustrated in Plates LII to LXVII, as they stand loosely associated according to some central idea; and it may be just as well not to wander overmuch into a consideration of others that are known to exist, but simply to use those reproduced as indications of what the diligent collector may expect to find, once in a way, if his luck is good. Such a chapter will necessarily be somewhat disconnected and disjointed, but this is, I fear, inevitable.

In the whole history of Britain the most romantic family is that of the Stuarts, the kingly race whose vicissitudes of fortune and vagaries of personality are as remarkable as the amazing sentiment of loyalty that they seem to have been always able to inspire; and there is perhaps no more pathetic chapter, even in their records, than that devoted to their ill-omened attempts to regain the crowns they had lost. How far, at any rate after

Jacobitism and its Relics.

ENGLISH TABLE GLASS

A.D. 1715, the Jacobite faith was anything more than a sentiment, cannot be discussed here; or what chances there might have been of the ultimate triumph of the cause, had its leaders been in any way worthy of the devotion lavished on them. But it is well known that the cause of the white rose had very many staunch adherents, and that even among the ranks of the Hanoverians there were those who looked, with a sympathy only half veiled, on their neighbours who drank to "the king over the water." It was in the north and west of England, and in the marches of Wales (not to speak of the highlands of Scotland), that the tradition was long cherished; and it is from the English counties, thus loyal to old memories, that most of the glasses which bear Jacobite emblems come: frail mementoes of a long-lost cause, which have outlasted by many scores of years the devotion of its followers and the fascination of its leaders. To them, as to all other relics of dead days and forgotten hopes, there clings a feeling of gentle melancholy; they bring us memories of gallant gentlemen to whom they crystallized a life's ideal, and they are eloquent of that tenacious and affectionate fidelity that even the most

PLATE LII

INSCRIBED GLASSES, BEARING JACOBITE MOTTOES
AND EMBLEMS.
201. Height, 6¼ inches. **200.** **202.** Height, 6⅜ inches.

INSCRIBED GLASSES

worthless of the fickle Stuarts could always command. Most of the Jacobite glasses are memorials of the second attempt to regain the throne of Britain, the famous "forty-five;" but there are a few which have reference to that of A.D. 1715, and No. 200 is an example of this group. As will be seen, it bears (executed with the diamond) the cypher of the "Old Pretender," *I.R.* beneath a crown, and within a beautiful border two verses of the Jacobite song, "God save the King," which was afterwards paraphrased into the Hanoverian National Anthem. The second verse runs thus—

The Two Rebellions.

> *God Bliss the Prince of Wales,*
> *The True born Prince of Wales,*
> *Sent us by Thee.*
> *Grant us one favour more,*
> *The King for to Restore,*
> *As Thou hast done before,*
> *The Familie.*

Mr. Albert Hartshorne, in his elaborate and most interesting chapter on Jacobite glasses, records six others of this type, and as these are all in the possession of families who treasure them, there is but little chance of the amateur finding one; still, there is always the possibility of one turning up,

ENGLISH TABLE GLASS

and the knowledge of the rarity of a desired example is the collector's strongest incentive. The fervour of the Jacobites was largely kept alive by means of private associations **Jacobite** of gentlemen, such as the famous **Clubs.** "Cycle Club;" and judging from the number of emblem-bearing glasses that survive, there must, undoubtedly, have been many of these associations. Their glasses bore various symbols and mottoes, but there is a generic likeness running through them all, from such simple and early pieces as No. 201, with its rose, two buds, and stem, to such elaborate examples as those which bore portraits of "Bonnie Prince Charlie," Virgilian quotations allusive to the cause, or such quaint and beautiful emblems as the stricken tree putting forth branches with the motto *Revirescit*. All these were frankly and completely incriminating had they come within the official ken of the Government; but there are others in which the allusions were veiled, and which we should not know for Jacobite had we not examples indubitably pertaining to that cult, to which their resemblance is clear. Such is No. 202, with its natural roses on the bowl and the heraldic rose and leaves beautifully engraved *under the foot*, a rare

PLATE LIII

INSCRIBED GLASSES, BEARING JACOBITE MOTTOES
AND EMBLEMS.

204. Height, $6\frac{1}{8}$ inches.   203. Height, $7\frac{1}{4}$ inches.   205. Height, 6 inches.

PLATE LIV

INSCRIBED GLASSES, BEARING JACOBITE MOTTOES
AND EMBLEMS.
207. Height, 7⅛ inches. 206. Height, 8⅝ inches. 208. Height, 6⅞ inches.

INSCRIBED GLASSES

and early piece, two of which I found in Bristol. Glasses like this, and such pieces as Nos. 210 and 211, which bear badges not undeniably Jacobite, might have been used by the more discreet adherents to the cause, such as the cunning wit who was reproached for not praying for the king, and answered, "For the King I do pray, but I do not think it necessary to tell God who is the King."

We know that the creed of Jacobitism (however much it may have degenerated from a living force into a mere tradition) flourished through a long series of years; and this duration of its vitality is reflected in the extended sequence of the glasses that bear the emblems. Starting with the plain-stemmed pieces of early date, allusive to the rising of 1715, we find air twists, an occasional outside twist (No. 205), white twists, and cut stems; while the list is closed by glasses of the types which belong to the very end of the eighteenth century. Very few of these glasses are immediately contemporary with the moving events of the struggle; nearly all of them belong to the years after 1745, and stand to-day as records of an unceasing adherence to a gradually dying cause.

ENGLISH TABLE GLASS

The most important are probably the portrait glasses, which fall naturally into two groups, those which bear the presentment of the "Old Pretender," and those showing the likeness of his son, "Bonnie Prince Charlie." Of the former class is No. 206, with the mottoes "COGNOSCUNT ME MEI" and "PREMIUM VIRTUTIS," a glass which is purely commemorative: of the latter Nos. 203 and 209 are types. No. 203 bears, in addition to the *pseudo* likeness of the "Young Pretender," the rose and thistle with the Jacobite star and the Cycle motto, "*Fiat*"; while 209 is decorated with flags, military emblems, and the motto "AB OBICE MAJOR," as well as with the portrait in a panel. This, with its cut stem and elaborate engraving, is not improbably as late as A.D. 1788, and must accordingly be considered a personal memorial of Prince Charles Edward, made at a time when Jacobitism had ceased to be anything but a legend.

Portrait Glasses.

Much more frequent than the examples which are adorned with portraits are those which bear the simple emblems and their accompanying "word." Of these the star and the motto, "*Fiat*," associated with the national badges of the

Other Mottoes and Emblems.

PLATE LV

INSCRIBED GLASSES, BEARING JACOBITE MOTTOES
AND EMBLEMS.

210. Height, 5⅞ inches. **209.** Height, 7⅞ inches. **211.** Height, 5⅞ inches.

INSCRIBED GLASSES

rose and the thistle, have been mentioned as being Jacobite badges; but other "words" and emblems also occur—"*Redeat*," for instance (as on No. 208), bears an obvious reference to the hoped-for return of the king; and "RADIAT" (as on No. 212), a pursuing variant of this, being possibly allusive to the shining star of the creed. Rarer are "AUDENTIOR IBO," "TURNO TEMPUS ERIT," "GOD BLESS THE PRINCE," and "REDDAS INCOLUMEM"; and all these mottoes are to be found associated with differing selections and arrangements of the emblems.

The badges on No. 204, for instance, are the natural rose, the star, and the forget-me-not (a simple and beautiful piece of symbolism); on Nos. 205 and 207 are found the rose and the oak-leaf; on No. 208 the rose and the star; on Nos. 210 and 211 the rose and the thistle; and on No. 212 the royal arms of Great Britain. Whether the oak-leaf is allusive to the adventure of King Charles II in the Royal Oak, a part of the Stuart cult, is not certain; it may be so, or it might equally justly be suggested that English Jacobites used the oak-leaf and Scottish ones the thistle; the rose (as generally represented) with two buds being

ENGLISH TABLE GLASS

supposed to symbolise King James II and the Old and Young Pretenders.

It is not to be supposed that while the Jacobites proclaimed their disaffection on **Hanoverian Glasses.** their glasses, their opponents in power would refrain from some similar avowal of their political predilections; and glasses bearing Royalist sentiments still remain as evidence of the feeling of the Hanoverian's supporters. That they are less numerous than the others may possibly be due to the fact that the victors, possessing the spoils, had less need of nursing their rancour than the strong minority whose creed was under a ban. But it is curious to note that Hanoverian glasses exist of an earlier date than any Jacobite examples; No. 214, for instance, which bears *in relief* on the upper part of the four-sided stem the words, "God save King George." This piece dates from the reign of King George I; indeed, Mr. Hartshorne records a specimen of somewhat similar type (though more elaborately decorated) which bears the date 1716.

But the most fervid loyalty, or rather the **The Orangemen's Toast.** most aggressive opposition to the Stuart cause, was to be found in the north of Ireland, where the

PLATE LVI

INSCRIBED GLASSES, BEARING JACOBITE AND
LOYAL MOTTOES AND EMBLEMS.

212. Height, 6¾ inches. 213. Height, 8¼ inches. 214. Height, 6¾ inches.

INSCRIBED GLASSES

renown of King William III is enshrined in the hearts of all Orangemen. No Orange glasses appear to exist which are of an earlier date than the middle of the eighteenth century, so that they, like the Jacobite examples, were tokens of an inherited creed rather than the outcome of contemporary events; but they are interesting as showing that alongside the placid loyalty of the Hanoverian party there existed a group of gentlemen of militant convictions as staunch to the memory of Dutch William as were the Jacobites to the side of the Stuarts. No. 213 is a Williamite glass bearing the inscription—"THE IMORTAL MEMORY;" others read, "TO THE GLORIOUS MEMORY OF KING WILLIAM"—words from the Orange toast which begins, "To the glorious, pious, and immortal memory of the great and good King William, who freed us from Pope and Popery, knavery and slavery, brass money and wooden shoes," and concludes, after much inconsequent verbiage, with the hope that he who refuses the toast may be "damned, crammed, and rammed down the great gun of Athlone."

Among the more moderate men party rancour and dissension probably gave way gradually to national and patriotic ideals,

ENGLISH TABLE GLASS

Loyalty and Patriotism. crystallizing round the established sovereignty of the Guelphs, and this sentiment seems to have inspired the decoration of No. 215. Here the motto, "LIBERTY," is associated with the rose of England and the white horse of Hanover, and in the next example (No. 217) the national ideal of a united kingdom seems to be expressed by the intertwined rose and thistle and the Union Jack (without the cross of St. Patrick) encircled by the motto of the Order of the Garter. Still another phase of political belief in a time of continuous Continental warfare, that of peaceful patriotism, pure and simple, is probably responsible for the figure of Britannia bearing the olive branch, engraved with great skill on No. 218, and on a rummer of the same date in Mrs. Rees Price's cabinet. With these is naturally associated the decanter reproduced in Plate XLIII, bearing national emblems and the toast, "THE LAND WE LIVE IN," a sentiment with which few could be found to disagree. The other glass illustrated in Plate LVII is associated with those of royalist and national inspiration, as it records the coronation of King George IV, bearing the date "JULY 19, 1821," and the picturesque figure of the King's Champion.

PLATE LVII

INSCRIBED GLASSES, BEARING LOYAL AND
PATRIOTIC EMBLEMS.

215. Height, 6⅜ inches. 216. Height, 6 inches. 218. Height, 6⅝ inches.
217. Height, 5⅝ inches.

INSCRIBED GLASSES

In this connection it may be interesting to mention a monument of disloyalty, a tumbler formerly in the possession of an old friend of mine. It bore on one side the word "TINKER," and on the other the word "KING," and concealed in the ornaments below the latter were several slits, so that if the person drinking chose the Tinker as his toast the liquor arrived at its proper destination, but if in loyal custom he toasted the King, the ale would pour through the perforations, not only failing to reach his lips, but drenching him into the bargain.

It is not a long step from devotion to the sentiment of national greatness to admiration of the men who were responsible for raising the country to the climax of victory; and this— *Heroes— Naval and Military.* one might almost say—adoration of the hero of the moment is found recorded on perishable glass as well as the triple brass of more enduring memorials of a nation's love. Nelson's memory was not infrequently thus honoured; some glasses bear his portrait, others his famous flagship the "Victory," and yet others (see No. 219) his funeral car and catafalque adorned with the name of his two great triumphs of "TRAFALGAR" and the

ENGLISH TABLE GLASS

"NILE." The popular worship of another naval leader, Admiral Keppel, is evinced on No. 220, a tumbler which owes its origin to the wave of appreciation that passed over the country after his trial and acquittal in 1779; and as this gallant sailor was created a viscount in 1782 this glass (obviously dating between those years) is valuable as a standard of style and decoration by which to fix the date of such examples as No. 221, bearing the same characteristic ornamentation.

Yet another naval glass, that was once in my possession, and now rests in Mr. Singer's collection, bears round the rim the names "DUNCAN, ST. VINCENT, HOWE, NELSON," a relic of the admiration entertained by its unknown owner for the great leaders whose names are thus recorded.

With all the British pride in the Navy, the claims of military men to recognition were not disregarded by the engravers of the period; and while in the nineteenth century, "*Wellington for ever*" was emblazoned over a sword, as in No. 222 (the bird of peace being engraved on the other side of the bowl), fifty years earlier our friends on the Continent were not neglected. Whoever drank from No. 223, or from a glass in my own cabinet similarly

PLATE LVIII

INSCRIBED GLASSES, COMMEMORATING NATIONAL HEROES
220. Height, 3⅞ inches. 219. Height, 8¼ inches. 221. Height, 3¾ inches.

PLATE LIX

INSCRIBED GLASSES, COMMEMORATING NATIONAL
HEROES, Etc.
223. Height. 7⅞ inches. 222. Height, 4⅞ inches. 224. Height, 7⅝ inches.

INSCRIBED GLASSES

inscribed, pledged the great Frederick, King of Prussia, a sovereign whose popularity in this country dated from the battle of Rossbach, where he destroyed a French army, with the result that he was bonfired and belauded all over the kingdom as the "Protestant hero."

An interesting example, with the curious inscription, "*De Negotie*, Anno 1772," is figured as No. 224. It has been suggested that these words refer **A Cryptic Inscription.** to the judgment delivered in that year in the case of the slave Somerset, who, after being arrested as a fugitive, was liberated by order of the Courts on the ground that a slave became a free man as soon as he stepped on British soil. This is probably a glass made in Bristol, a great Quaker centre, and a port nearly connected by ties of trade with the slave-holding provinces of America, and it is not unlikely that some member of the Society of Friends had the rummer engraved (by the diamond-point) with this inscription, commemorating a notable step in the anti-slavery crusade.

The bitterness of political feeling all through the eighteenth century is well known, and the stubborn way in which Parliamentary elections were fought, with

ENGLISH TABLE GLASS

lavish bribery and unscrupulous corruption,
Political and Parliamentary. is a matter of history; so that it is little wonder that a few glasses still bear records of these heated contests. Nos. 225 and 226 are cider glasses, both bear apple-trees on the bowl, and the former has also the motto "NO EXCISE," the farmer's protest against the taxation of his home-brewed drink, which has already been alluded to; while No. 227, an interesting piece in the collection of Mr. J. T. Cater, commemorates the still unforgotten upheaval caused in the country by Wilkes and the famous No. 45 of his "North Briton." This story need not be repeated here, and no comment need be made on No. 229, with the inscription "SIR I POLE FOR EVER," probably a relic of some fiercely contested election; while No. 228, a fragment of glass of a type somewhat resembling No. 1, also bears an inscription referring to a Parliamentary election, which seems to have been a political cataclysm not mentioned in our histories. It reads "THE REVOLUTION OF Lowth, Novemb^r the 1st, 1755," and is said to commemorate the triumph of a loyal and independent club in returning Mr. Thomas Tipping to Parliament; a change, doubtless, but one—however

PLATE LX

INSCRIBED GLASSES, BEARING POLITICAL AND
SOCIAL MOTTOES, ETC.

225. Height, 6⅛ inches. **227.** Height, 6⅞ inches. **230.** Height, 6⅝ inches.
226. Height, 6⅞ inches. **228.** Height, 1¾ inches. **229.** Height, 6¾ inches.

INSCRIBED GLASSES

complete—which was only a "revolution," so far as Louth itself was concerned.

Comparatively few glasses of the eighteenth century bear inscriptions which relate to the highly convivial and bibulous habits of the time; possibly had the idea of thus perpetuating these characteristics occurred to any of the "three-bottle" heroes of old, they would have deemed the surviving glasses themselves quite as convincing to future generations as any record or inscription. But some few seem to have thought otherwise, and to have chosen to inscribe their favourite glasses with symbol or with sentiment embodying their roystering creed and custom. Of the glasses so treated, the first on my list is No. 230, an example reasonably accorded priority because of the unusual nature of the society it belonged to. Among the multiplicity of the Glasgow clubs of the eighteenth century (concerning which a large and thick octavo has been compiled) surely this body was unique, for it was indeed a "sober" club, and the members drank at their meetings nothing but water. This particular glass was the property of Alexander Allan, of Newhall, the "PROVOST ALLEN" of No. 235, and is now in the

Convivial and Masonic.

possession of Major F. W. Allan, a leading light of Scottish Freemasonry, P.G.M. of his province, and a true exponent of the honourable principles of the craft. Fitly balancing No. 235 therefore, on Plate LXI, is an English masonic firing-glass, once the property of John Boulderson, of Falmouth; while other masonic glasses are figured as Nos. 238 and 240, the latter bearing the name of "MOTHER KILWINNING," the lodge which, on the score of antiquity, obtains and is accorded precedence of all other Scottish lodges.

How often from this quaint little example the toast of "King and Craft" has been **Toasts and** drunk with all the honours due, **Sentiments.** no man can say. Masonry has its social side, as well as its moral and benevolent purpose, and it is popularly believed that neither is neglected; certainly this glass was made for use, and was used, as is evident from the fragment broken and replaced. Another Scottish specimen is No. 231, which bears the rather mysterious words, "THE BLACK FACE O'T" round the rim; and balancing this is an English example (No. 232), on which—associated with a figure of Mercury and other commercial

PLATE LXI

INSCRIBED GLASSES, BEARING SOCIAL MOTTOES
AND TOASTS.
231. Height, 3⅔ inches. 233. Height, 7⅜ inches. 232. Height, 4¼ inches.
234. Height, 4 inches. 235. Height, 4½ inches.

PLATE LXII

INSCRIBED GLASS, BEARING THE ARMS AND
MOTTO OF THE TURNERS' COMPANY
OF LONDON.

236. Height, 9¾ inches.

INSCRIBED GLASSES

emblems—we find the sentiment, "*As we travel through life may we live well on the road.*" Both these glasses probably belong to the early years of the nineteenth century, but it nevertheless seemed worth while to include them here.

Some of the most interesting glasses inscribed with toasts are those which bear the names of ladies, reigning beauties who were the idols of their day and generation. Mr. Albert Hartshorne possesses one inscribed, "*Mrs. Walpole, June 27th 1716,*" which doubtless comes into this class; and No. 233 is not impossibly of the same character, bearing as it does the name "MRS. A. GOF."

At Levens Hall is preserved a tall glass of the early years of the eighteenth century which Mr. Hartshorne described as "inscribed round the rim LEVENS HIGH CONSTABLE," and used time out of mind at the *Radish Feast* to drink the mysterious "Morocco," and "Luck to Levens as long as the Kent flows." This is a ceremonial glass, and No. 236 would seem to fall into the same category—a very handsome piece, elaborately engraved with the arms, crest, and motto of the Turners'

Societies, Hunts, and Clubs.

Company of London. This may have been so decorated for an enthusiastic Turner, or it may have been a Master's cup, or even a loving-cup—in any case, it brings to mind the quaint toast given at the Company's Livery Dinner: "The pretty maids, the merry wives, and the buxom widows of the Turners' Company." In this connection a passing allusion may be made to No. 243, a tumbler of much later date, which bears the arms of the Bakers' Company.

The cheerful toper who inscribed on a glass possessed by Mrs. Rees Price, "*Wine does wonders every day,*" was probably a sportsman of the old school, who would have delighted in the mighty goblet now in the same collection which bears (with a beautifully engraved vine pattern) a decidedly adipose figure of Bacchus astride a barrel with a goblet in each hand, and the triumphant declaration, "JOVE DECREED THE GRAPE SHOULD BLEED FOR ME." He might perhaps have been a member of the "Confederate Hunt" (a Welsh club with lady patronesses, which, at any rate, existed from 1754 to 1758), or possibly a follower of "THE FRIENDLY HUNT," whose little glass is figured as No. 239; in any case, he would

PLATE LXIII

INSCRIBED GLASSES, BEARING SOCIAL MOTTOES
AND EMBLEMS.

238. Height, 2¼ inches. 237. Height, 6⅞ inches. 240. Height, 3 inches.
239. Height, 3⅝ inches.

INSCRIBED GLASSES

have found himself at home with the roystering gentlemen who are depicted (engraved and gilt) on No. 237, with their motto, "KEEP IT UP," or among the eccentric souls to whom the quaint symbols on No. 241 had a meaning. To the observer of to-day the reason for the choice of a cat as the instrumentalist, and the bagpipe as the instrument, is far from clear; and the connection of this grotesque with the motto, "HONOUR AND FRIENDSHIP," is still less obvious.

Glasses inscribed to naval heroes have already been alluded to; now we come to the cases in which the inscription refers to the ship, and not particularly to the man. *Ship and Naval Glasses.* The first of these to be illustrated is a very notable example (figured as No. 242), a tumbler on which are engraved the words, "Succefs to the BRITANNIA, EDM^D ECCLESTON, 1774"; and this is a piece which is further interesting as still possessing the original cover. Other specimens of this same group are reproduced on Plate LXV, and one which always delights me is No. 247, inscribed "SUCCESS TO THE BRITISH FLEET, 1759" (referring to Hawke's defeat of the French at Quiberon

Bay, on November 20 of that year), and engraved with the quaintest old ships heaving and tossing on the oddest and curliest of waves, as well as a figure of Britannia analogous to that on No. 218. The tall glass figured as No. 244, which bears the toast, "*Succefs to the Renown*" (a name not unknown in the Navy), also possesses considerable interest; but it is when we come to Nos. 245 and 246 that we are brought into touch with another phase of the eighteenth century, a custom long dead so far as Britain is concerned. The former, over the gallant ship in full sail with the long pennon, is inscribed, " Success to the EAGLE FRIGATE, JOHN KNILL COMMANDER," and it is puzzling to learn from the Navy Papers that during the eighteenth century no King's ship named the *Eagle* was under the command of a John Knill; but the second piece, with its toast, " Success to the LYON Privateer," gives the clue, and shows that these very charming examples are relics of the old days when privateering was a very lucrative speculation. Dampier, on one voyage, secured booty to the value of nearly £200,000; and while we know nothing of the *Eagle's* record in this respect, we know at least that

PLATE LXIV

INSCRIBED GLASSES, BEARING SOCIAL AND NAVAL MOTTOES AND EMBLEMS.
241. Height, 5¾ inches.   242. Height, 6¼ inches.   243. Height, 4¾ inches.

PLATE LXV

INSCRIBED GLASSES, BEARING NAVAL TOASTS
AND DESIGNS.

244. Height, 8 inches.   **245.** Height, 6⅝ inches.   **247.** Height, 7⅞ inches.
                   246. Height, 6¼ inches.

INSCRIBED GLASSES

she made more than one voyage, for other glasses exist in which she is toasted without her commander's name being stated. Bristol was a great privateering port; in that city these glasses were bought and probably made; and one is perhaps justified in concluding that they were Bristol vessels which were thus toasted.

In few cases has the personal note a quainter and more abiding charm; in few instances is the glass more redolent of old times and old habits than in one or two of the pieces illustrated on Plate LXVI. The glass figured as No. 249, inscribed, "I. PADWICK DEAN," simply records the ownership of a forgotten worthy; but Nos. 248 (c. 1740) and 251 (of a later date) tell us something of his individual tastes; for "P: TATE," the possessor (otherwise unknown to fame) of the former, was clearly a devotee of the fiddle, a jovial soul to whom melody and Malmsey were both delights; while "TOM SHORTER," whose counterfeit presentment is seen on his glass, hunting the red deer with horse and hounds, was evidently one of the old Exmoor sportsmen, immortalized—at least, while this glass endures—on the frailest of materials.

Names of Owners.

ENGLISH TABLE GLASS

Sometimes one finds simply the owner's cypher on a glass, sometimes his crest, sometimes even more elaborate marks of possession. No. 250, for instance, bears a quaintly engraved coat-of-arms, and the words, "A-SQ^r BECKFORD," but this Beckford was not the millionaire collector and romancer of "Vathek" fame; and I have a rummer with a cut stem inscribed " CHARLOTTE HAYWARD BORN MARCH THE 9, 1774," which (like a tumbler of later date in my cabinet, with an analogous inscription) would seem to have taken the place of the more familiar "christening mug."

Let me record a wine glass with a beautiful white spiral stem, on the bowl of which are engraved the words, "*Brid^t Alderson to Ann Brooks.*" It seems a curious present for one lady to make another, and I wonder if the friendship were half as enduring as the glass.

Let me conclude this section with a description of Nos. 252, 253, and 254, three **Emblem Glasses.** of the most interesting pieces in my cabinet; glasses of singularly fine metal, decorated with excellent engraving, which may possibly date from A.D. 1730. It will be seen that each bears a motto

PLATE LXVI

INSCRIBED GLASSES, BEARING DIVERS NAMES
AND ALLUSIVE DESIGNS.

250. Height, 6⅛ inches.   248. Height, 6 inches.   251. Height, 5⅞ inches.
                          249. Height, 6½ inches.

INSCRIBED GLASSES

associated with an emblem in a panel. To the representation of bees hovering over flowers is appended the line, "*Hence we gather our Sweets.*" "*I elevate what I confume*" relates to a heart tried by fire; while the palm-tree growing on a rugged rock seems to say, "*I rife by difficulties.*" Each is what old Quarles called a "moral emblem," and the sentiment of all is unimpeachable; but the man for whom these glasses were made had the brain of a subtle humorist under his periwig, for the mottoes not only refer to the pictured symbols, but also bear a less obvious relation to the glass, the wine, and the drinker. The first may be taken as the wine-lover's allusion to the sweets to be imbibed from the glass; the second to the action of raising the glass in a toast; while the third might surely be understood, without undue straining, as referring to the condition of the drinker after numerous and deep libations, and be read, "*I rise with difficulty!*"

* * * * *

My tale is told; I fear, with many and great imperfections in the telling, but honestly

ENGLISH TABLE GLASS

Valedictory. and to the best of my ability. If I have succeeded in conveying to my readers some little information on the subject of a singularly interesting series of objects, I am content; if I have suggested, however incompletely, something of the charm and fascination that our old glasses have for the seeing eye and the sympathetic mind, I am, indeed, more than satisfied.

All glass is frail and brittle, and much that was worthy of the most careful preservation has already passed to destruction; all the more does it behove all who care for relics of our ancestor's good taste, their creeds, their passions, and their personality, to cherish all that remain, eloquent as they are of memories of dead days, some proud, some sad, some foolish, but all intensely interesting. The man who destroys an old example destroys a fragment of history, the miscreant who attempts to forge one wrongs our forebears as well as ourselves, and the erring soul who places on a long-descended glass an inscription of to-day, is only a little less culpable, even when he writes with as apt an artificiality as the rhymester who scratched on an old rummer—

INSCRIBED GLASSES, BEARING PICTORIAL EMBLEMS AND MOTTOES.
252. Height, 6⅜ inches.   **253.** Height, 6⅜ inches.   **254.** Height, 6⅜ inches.

INSCRIBED GLASSES

In this old glass, in other times more debonair and gay
  Than our dull decent plodding hours that mock us as they pass,
Wit lurked and flashed (though often drowned), and song and laughter lay
    In this old glass.

What if the men who quaffed from it their golden Hippocras
Are but a mellow memory now, sans rhyme or roundelay?
Their jovial ghosts are with us still, though o'er them grows the grass.

These bid us smile: and though the years our temples touch to grey,
  And though ambition's clarion call becomes but sounding brass,
Old love endures, old wine is ours—pledge me, old friend to-day,
    In this old glass.

INDEX

ADAMS, an English glass decorator, 87

Air-twist stems: ale glasses, 60-62; rummers, 67; "tears," or bubbles, in, 40; wine glasses, 27, 28, 39, 40, 42-46

Ale glasses: air-twist (Nos. 121-123, 125, 126), Plates xxviii, xxix, xxx, 60, 61, 62; baluster stems (Nos. 116-118), Plate xxvii, 58, 59; cut stems (No. 127), Plate xxx, 62; plain stems (Nos. 119, 120), Plate xxviii, 59, 60; white twist stems (No. 124), Plate xxix, 61; smaller pieces like (Nos. 109, 249), Plates xxv, lxvi, 55, 62, 118; yard-of-ale glass (No. 145), Plate xxxviii, 62, 63, 71; bulb at the base, its supposed object, 63; some modern reproductions, 64; interesting seventeenth-century ale glass (No. 116), Plate xxvii, 58; specimens with folded foot, 59; specimen in the possession of a Brighton collector, 59; funnel-shaped specimen on which is engraved "Disher's Ale," 61

Allan, Alexander, of Newhall (the provost), alluded to, 111

Allan, Major F. W., specimens belonging to (Nos. 230, 235), Plates lx, lxi, 110, 112

Arms: Arundell (?) (No. 191), Plate xlix, 82, 84; Bakers' Company (No. 243), Plate lxiv, 114, 116; Turners' Company (No. 236), Plate lxii, 113; royal arms (No. 212), Plate lvi, 104

Athlone, the great gun of, alluded to, 105

BAKERS' Company, of London, arms of the (No. 243), Plate lxiv, 114

Baluster stems: ale glasses, 58, 59; goblets, 64, 65; "tears," or bubbles, in, 33; wine glasses, 27, 32-35

Bath, city of, alluded to, 6, 15, 61

Beckford, William, of Fonthill, alluded to, 118

Bell, with trailed decoration (No. 181), Plate xlvi, 79, 80

"Bonnie Prince Charlie." *See* Jacobites

Borde, Andrew (Merry Andrew), physician to Henry VIII, alluded to, 5

Bottles. *See* Decanters

Boulderson, John, of Falmouth, glass formerly belonging to (No. 234), Plate lxi, 112

Bowes, Sir Jerome, an early glass-maker, alluded to, 23

Bowl (covered), with trailed decoration (No. 182), Plate xlvii, 80

Bowls, varieties and types of, 30, 41; classification, 30, 31; expansion of the lip, *ib.*; ogee from Bristol houses, 51; straight-sided, *ib.*; associated with air-twist stems, *ib.*

Box, near Bath, the Queen's Head at, 71

Braintree, an example from, 70

Brighton, alluded to, 59

Bristol, alluded to, 6, 79, 84, 101, 109, 117; single ogee-bowl largely made at, 36, 51; coloured twists made at, 54; example of ale glass purchased at (No. 127), Plate xxx, 61

Britannia, medallion of, on wine glass (No. 218), Plate lvii, 56, 106

British Museum, tankard which belonged to William Cecil, Lord Burleigh, at, 21; illustrations of specimens at, Plate ii, 22; (Nos. 193, 194), Plate l, 86; (No. 206),

British Museum—*continued.*
Plate liv, 101; (No. 209), Plate lv, 102; (No. 213), Plate lvi, 104; (No. 229), Plate lx, 110; (No. 249), Plate lxvi, 118
Bromley, Kent, alluded to, 63
Buckingham, Duke of, his furnaces at Greenwich, alluded to, 23
Burleigh, William Cecil, Lord, his glass tankard at the British Museum, 21
Burns, Robert, poem by, engraved on goblet, 85
Byng, Admiral, commemorated on a glass, 12

CANDLESTICKS, also a series, 74; (Nos. 165–167), Plate xli, *ib.*
Carlisle, " Joey " glasses from (Nos. 148, 149), Plate xxxviii, 71
Carlyle, Thomas, quoted, 3
Cater, Mr. J. T., specimens in his possession (No. 172), Plate xliii, 76; (No. 227), Plate lx, 110
Charles II, description of seventeenth-century goblet, with portrait of, 23; alluded to, 8, 103
Charles Edward, Prince. *See* Jacobites
Cider glasses (Nos. 133, 225, 226), Plates xxxiv, lx, 67, 68, 110
Classification : typical and individual examples, 17; method of, 26; bowl types and nomenclature, 30; tendency to expansion of lip, 31; feet, three classes of, 28; second class without fold but with pontil-mark, 29; third class, pontil-mark polished away, 29; feet either conical or domed, 30; domed feet only found in association with baluster and rarely with air-twist stems, *ib.*; stems, five groups of, 27; air-twist, *ib.*; baluster, *ib.*; cut stem, *ib.*; plain stem, *ib.*; white twist stem, *ib.*; types of bowls not confined to wine glasses, 31; vessels without stems, *ib.*; flutes, yards, etc., *ib.*

Clubs : Confederate Hunt, 114; Cycle, 100; Jacobite, 101; " Sober Club," 111
Coins enclosed in " tears," or bubbles, 34
Collecting, the growing taste for, 2; possible to those of moderate means, *ib.*; beginning of the author's collection, 5; a fascinating pursuit to the thoughtful and artistic, 10, 11; warning concerning yard-of-ale glasses, 64; forgeries, frauds, and fakes, 18, 22, 53, 88–92, 95; pitfalls and problems, 93
Collar, the, 42, 43, 78; a prevailing feature of air-twist stems, 44
Coloured twist stems, 53
Coloured wine glasses, their rarity, 54
Confederate Hunt Club, alluded to, 114
Cosway, Richard, alluded to, 2
Covered cups intended more for display than use, 80
Crofts, J., 2nd Life Guards, 85
Crutched Friars, Jacob Verzelini's factory at, 20
Cut stems : ale glasses, 62; rummers, 67; wine glasses, 27, 28, 55, 56
" Cycle Club," a Jacobite association, 100; its motto, 102

DAMPIER, CAPTAIN WILLIAM, alluded to, 116
Decanters (Nos. 170, 172), Plates xlii, xliii, 75, 76; one used at the coronation of George IV, *ib.*
Decoration : the eighteenth century, although under-rated, noted for its artistic productions, 4; the metal and the engraving, 56; probable effects of the Regency on artistic crafts, 57; hop and barley decoration on ale glasses (Nos. 118, 124, 125), Plates xxvii, xxix, xxx, 58, 59, 61, 62, 82, 84; the conventional rose, 73; some

INDEX

Decoration—*continued*.
of the patterns, 82; methods (Nos. 184-192), Plate xlix, 82; varieties of engraving, 81; gilding and enamelling, 83; diamond-point engraving, 84; fluoric acid etching (Nos. 193, 194), Plate l, 86; Bacchus and his vine, 87, 114; impressed seals, 87

Dickens, Charles, alluded to, 24

"Disher's Ale" inscribed on funnel-shaped glasses, 61

Dram and spirit glasses (Nos. 150-164), Plates xxxix, xl, 69, 72, 73; a tiny specimen, 66

Drane, Mr., of Cardiff, his advice to collectors, 7; his collection of spoons, 9

Drawn glasses (Nos. 40-62), Plates xi-xv, 40-44; (Nos. 146-149), Plate xxxviii, 71; drawn stem goblets, 66

Drinking glass made in London by Jacob Verzelini, Plate ii, 20-22; drinking glasses numerous in the eighteenth century, 25

Drinking habits of the eighteenth century, 24

Dutch artists and examples, alluded to, 7, 51, 87, 91, 94

"EAGLE," the, a supposed privateer, 116

Edward IV, alluded to, 8

Elizabeth, Queen, her glass at Windsor Castle, 20

Elizabethan early English glasses, 20

Emblems inscribed on glass (Nos. 252, 253, 254), Plate lxvii, 118-120

Engraving, 56; varieties of, 81; patterns, 82; diamond-point, 84; Greenwood, 87; Wickenden, 85

"Evelyn's Diary," yard-glasses mentioned in, 63

Exmoor, alluded to, 12, 117

FALMOUTH, alluded to, 112

Fashion, change and development, an interesting study, 8

Feet, three classes of wine glasses, 28, 29; conical or domed, 30; their character on forgeries, 88, 89; engraved upon underneath, 83, 100; folded feet on ale glasses, 59; in pieces with trailed decoration, 80; on goblets, 66; on wine glasses, 28, 35, 36-38, 51, 52

Fluoric acid, decoration by means of, 86

Foreign work compared with English eighteenth-century glass, 1; not easily distinguished from English productions, 94

Forgeries, frauds, and fakes, 18, 22; pontil-mark sometimes removed, 53; feet and their characteristics, 88, 89; (Nos. 195-198), Plate li, 89; stems and spirals, 90; a so-called "Williamite" glass, 91; importance of noting colour of the metal, 92; pitfalls and problems, 93; summary, 95

Foster, Felix, an early decorator of glass, 85

Franklin, Benjamin, his glass alluded to, 72

Frederick the Great, alluded to, 109

French defeat at Rossbach, alluded to, 109; inscribed glass commemorating defeat by Admiral Hawkes (No. 247), Plate lxv, 115, 116, 117

Frome, alluded to, 13

GEORGE I, KING, alluded to, 104

George III, King, decorated glass said to have belonged to (No. 185), Plate xlix, 82, 86

George IV, King, decanter used at his coronation (No. 172), Plate xliii, 76; glass recording his coronation (No. 216), Plate lvii, 106

Germany, fluoric acid etching probably originated in, 86

Gilding and enamelling, 83

Giles of York, an early decorator of glass, 85

125

ENGLISH TABLE GLASS

Glasgow, alluded to, 15; rummer probably made in (No. 140), Plate xxxvi, 69; its clubs, 111

Goblets: seventeenth-century specimen with portraits of Charles II and his queen described, 23; stunted specimens from the Low Countries, 30; rare short-stemmed specimens, 62; with baluster stem (Nos. 128, 129), Plates xxxi, xxxii, 64, 65; of heroic size, *ib.*; drawn stem (No. 130), Plate xxxiii, 66; the folded foot on goblets, 66; glass of a bibulous patient, 66; specimen with poem by Burns engraved thereon, 85

Greene, John, glass-seller of London, alluded to, 23

Greenwich, the Duke of Buckingham's furnace at, alluded to, 23

Greenwood, an English decorator of glass (No. 193), Plate l, 87

Guelphs, the, alluded to, 106

HANOVERIAN National Anthem, second verse of, 99; Hanoverian glasses, 104

Hartshorne, Mr. Albert, F.S.A., his monograph on the subject, 9, 10; his method of classification, 26, 27 (*note*); quoted, 48; alluded to, 20, 21, 30, 49, 50, 54, 72, 77, 87, 99, 104, 113

Hawke, Admiral, his victory at Quiberon the subject of an inscription (No. 247), Plate lxv, 115, 117

Henry VIII, King, alluded to, 5

Holland, alluded to, 1, 36, 50, 51, 54, 86, 94; stunted goblets from, 30; glass-house referred to, 91

Hop and barley decoration, 58, 59, 61, 62, 82, 84

Houghton's "Letters for the Improvement of Trade and Husbandry," referred to, 25

Hume, Mr. Joseph, M.P., "Joeys" named after, 71

IMPRESSED seals, 87

Incised twist stems, wine glasses, 37, 38

Inscribed and historic glasses, 96; glasses bearing Jacobite mottoes and emblems (Nos. 200-214), Plates lii, 97, 98; liii. 100; liv, 101; lv, 102; lvi, 104; Jacobite emblems and traditions long cherished, 98; most Jacobite glasses memorials of the "forty-five," 99; Hanoverian National Anthem, 99; rose decoration (Nos. 201, 202), Plate lxii, 100; Jacobite clubs, 100; few specimens of Jacobite emblems immediately contemporary, 101; portrait glasses (Nos. 203, 206, 209), Plates liii, liv, lv, 100-102; Hanoverian glasses, 104; the Orangeman's Toast, 104; "Williamite" glass, 105; Orange glasses, 105; bearing loyal and patriotic mottoes and emblems (Nos. 215-218), Plate lvii, 106; Tinker and King glass, 107; heroes, naval and military, commemorated (Nos. 219-224), Plates lviii, lix, 107-109; a cryptic inscription, 109; rummer commemorating the anti-slavery crusade (No. 224), Plate lix, 109; "The revolution of Lowth" (No. 228), Plate lx, 110; arms of the Turners' Company (No. 236), Plate lxii, 113, 114; arms of the Bakers' Company (No. 243), Plate lxiv, 114; political, naval, and social mottoes, etc., toasts and emblems (Nos. 225-243), Plates lx, 110; lxi, 112; lxiii, 114; lxiv, 115, 116; bearing naval toasts and designs (Nos. 244-247), Plate lxv, 117; bearing divers names and allusive designs (Nos. 248-251), Plate lxvi, 118; bearing pictorial emblems and mottoes (Nos. 252-254), Plate lxvii, 120

INDEX

Inscriptions, mottoes, etc., on glasses, 12, 21, 87, 89, 93, 99–119

JACOBITES, alluded to, 11; specimen of glass in Mr. Singer's collection, 82; their relics, 97; emblems and traditions, long cherished, 98; memorials of the "forty-five," 99; clubs, 100; emblems and portraits, 101, 102; James Francis Edward, the "Old Pretender," 99, 102, 104; Charles Edward, "Bonnie Prince Charlie"—the "Young Pretender," 100, 102, 104; glasses inscribed with mottoes and emblems (Nos. 200–214), Plates lii, 98; liii, 100; liv, 101; lv, 102; lvi, 103, 104
James II, King, alluded to, 104; his health drunk in a yard-glass, 63
"Joey" glasses, or friends to temperance (No. 147), Plate xxxviii, 70, 71

KEPPEL, ADMIRAL, portrait and inscription (No. 220), Plate lviii, 108
King and craft toast, alluded to, 112
Knill, John, commander of the *Eagle* frigate, alluded to, 116

LAMERIE, PAUL, alluded to, 2
Lane, Mr. John, alluded to, 71
Levens Hall, eighteenth-century tall glass preserved at, 113
Liqueur glasses, 70 (Nos. 42, 74, 131), Plates xi, 40; xviii, 46; xxxiii, 66
Lorraine, "gentlemen glassmakers" from, alluded to, 22
Louth, a recorded revolution at (No. 228), Plate lx, 110, 111
Low Countries. *See* Holland
"Luck to Levens," the toast alluded to, 113
Lynn, glass-house at, alluded to, 52

MACDONALD, ADMIRAL ROBERTSON, glasses once in his possession engraved under the foot, 83
Mansel, Sir Robert, an early glassmaker, alluded to, 23
Masonic and convivial inscriptions on glasses (Nos. 225–235, 237–243), Plates lx, 110; lxi, 112; lxiii, 114; lxiv, 116
Mercury, the figure of, inscribed on Scottish specimen (No. 232), Plate lxi, 112
Merry Andrew. *See* Borde
Metal, 33, 39, 56; of forgeries, 91; colour of, 92
Mixed twist stems, wine glasses, 45, 47
"Morocco," strong ale used at the annual Radish Feast at Levens Hall, 113
Mugs, tankards, and tumblers (Nos. 136, 138, 140, 142–144, 220, 221, 243), Plates xxxv, 68; xxxvi, 69; xxxvii, 70; lviii, 108; lxiv, 116; tankard which belonged to William Cecil, Lord Burleigh, at the British Museum, 21

NATIONAL heroes, naval and military, recorded on glasses (Nos. 219–224), Plates lviii, 107, 108; lix, 109
Navy and ships, inscriptions relating to (Nos. 242, 244–247), Plates lxiv, 116; lxv, 117
Nelson, Lord, inscriptions relating to (No. 219), Plate lviii, 107, 108
Newhall, 111
Normandy, "gentlemen glassmakers" from, alluded to, 22
Norwich glass-house, a type of bowl supposed to have been made at (No. 91), Plate xxii, 51, 52

"OLD English Glasses," by Mr. Albert Hartshorne, alluded to, 10
"Old Pretender," the. *See* Jacobites

"Orange" glasses and "Orange" toasts, 104, 105

PENNSYLVANIA, the Historical Society of, Benjamin Franklin's glass alluded to, 72
Perry, Dr., inscribed glass belonging to (No. 200), Plate lii, 98, 99
Pevensey, old haunted house at, alluded to, 5
Photographing specimens, method of, 18, 19
Plain stems: ale glasses, 59, 60; rummers, 67; "tears," or bubbles, in, 35; wine glasses, 27, 34, 36–38
Political and Parliamentary inscriptions on glasses (Nos. 225–230), Plate lx, 110
Pontil-mark on forgeries, 53; on trailed decoration pieces, 80; alluded to, 29, 40, 46, 53, 56, 88, 89, 92
Porringer, two-handled, with trailed decoration (No. 183), Plate xlviii, 79, 81
Portraits engraved on glasses (Nos. 203, 206, 209), Plates liii, 100; liv, 101; lv, 102
Price, Mr. Rees, 15
Price, Mrs. Rees, her collection referred to, 15–17, 24, 53, 75, 84, 85, 89, 93, 106; specimens from her collection, Plates iv, 33; v, 34; vi, 35; vii, 36; viii, 37; ix, 38; x, 39; xi, 40; xii, 41; xiii, 42; xv, 44; xvi, 44; xvii, 45; xviii, 46; xix, 47; xx, 48; xxi, 50; xxii, 51; xxiii, 52; xxiv, 54; xxvi, 56; xxvii, 58; xxix, 61; xxx, 62; xxxiv, 67; xxxv, 68; xxxvi, 69; xxxvii, 70; xxxviii, 71; xxxix, 72; xli, 74; xlv, 78; xlvi, 79; xlvii, 80; xlix, 82; liii, 100; lv, 102; lvi, 104; lviii, 108; lix, 109; lx, 110; lxiii, 114; lxiv, 116

QUARLES, FRANCIS, alluded to, 119
Queen's Head at Bath, alluded to, 71
Quiberon Bay, Hawkes' defeat of the French at, commemorated, 115

"RADISH FEAST," the Leven, alluded to, 113
Rogers, Mrs., goblet presented to, 85
Rossbach, the battle of, alluded to, 109
"Royal Oak" glass, alluded to, 23
Rummers, the four types of stem, 67; plain stem (No. 132), Plate xxxiv, 67; air-twist stem (No. 133), *ib.*; white twist stem (No. 134), *ib.*; cut stem (No. 135), *ib.*; example commemorating the anti-slavery crusade (No. 224), Plate lix, 109

SEVENTEENTH century, English glass of the, 22
Singer, Mr. J. W., his experiences of collecting, 12, 13; allusion to pieces in his collection, 37, 54, 68, 72, 77, 82, 83, 108
Slave trade, a memorial of the, 109
Societies, hunts, and clubs, inscriptions relating to, 113
Somerset, the slave, a notable judgment relating to, commemorated on an inscribed glass, 109
Spanish example alluded to, 7
Spoon, the development of the, 8; Mr. Drane's collection of spoons alluded to, 9
Spirit glasses. *See* Dram and Spirit glasses
Stems: ale glasses, 59–62; coloured twist, 54; goblets, 62; rummers, 67; wine-glasses, 27; stems and spirals on forgeries, 90; the five groups of, 27; Plate i (*Frontispiece*)

INDEX

Sweetmeat glasses (Nos. 173-180), Plates xliii, 76; xliv, 77; xlv, 78; xlvi, 79

TANKARDS. *See* Mugs
"Tears," or bubbles, in baluster stems, Plates iii-vi, 32-36; in plain stems (No. 23), Plate vii, 35, 36; in air-twist stems (Nos. 42, 60, 85), Plates xi, xv, xx, 40, 44, 48
"Tinker and King" glass, a test of loyalty, 107
Tipping, Mr. Thomas, glass supposed to commemorate his election for Louth, 110
Toasts and sentiments inscribed on glasses (Nos. 237-240, 244-254), Plates lxiii, 112, 114; lxv, 117; lxvi, 118; lxvii, 120
Toddy fillers (Nos. 168, 169), Plate xlii, 75, 76
Trailed decoration pieces with, bell (No. 181), Plate xlvi, 79, 80; bowl (No. 182), Plate xlvii, 80; porringer (No. 183), Plate xlviii, 81
Travellers' glasses associated with the old coaching days (Nos. 146-164), Plates xxxviii, 71; xxxix, 72; xl, 73
Turners' Company of London, inscribed glass bearing the arms and motto of (No. 236), Plate lxii, 113, 114
Twist and stem, varieties of, 42
Two-handled cup (No. 136), Plate xxxv, 68

"VATHEK," alluded to, 118
Venetian glass, alluded to, 1, 7, 23
Venice, productions of English design made at, 23
Verzelini, Jacob, a Venetian worker in glass, 20, 21; drinking glass made by, Plate ii, 22; destruction of a splendid example of his work, *ib.*

WELLINGTON, DUKE OF, inscribed glass relating to (No. 222), Plate lix, 108
"Wemmick," his method suggestive of the habits of the early users of glasses, 24
White twist stems: ale glasses, 61; rummers, 67; wine glasses, 27, 48-52
Wickenden, J., engraver on glass, alluded to, 85
"Wilkes and Liberty," alluded to, 11; inscription on glass (No. 227), Plate lx, 110; Wilkes and the "North Briton," *ib.*
William III, King, alluded to, 105
William IV, King, alluded to, 8
"Williamite" glass (No. 213), Plate lvi, 104, 105; a forgery detected, 91
Windsor Castle, Queen Elizabeth's glass by Verzelini at, 20
Wine glasses: air-twist, drawn (Nos. 40-57), Plates xi, xii, xiii, xiv, 40-43; Plate i (*Frontispiece*), 27, 28; in some respects the most beautiful of English pieces, 39; fall into two groups, 39; method of manufacture, 40; their great popularity, *ib.*; air-twist, not drawn (Nos. 63-78), Plates xvi, 42, 44; xvii, 45; xviii, 46; xix, 47; persistency of type possibly due to conservatism of workmen, 43; a puzzling specimen (No. 65), Plate xvi, 43; the "collar" a prevalent feature of (Nos. 68, 69), Plate xvii, 44, 45; (Nos. 174, 236), Plates xliv, 77; lxii, 113; varieties of stem and bowl, 44; ornamentation of bowl, 45; feet with pontil-marks, 46; air-twist, with domed feet (Nos. 58-62), Plate xv, 44; baluster stem (Nos. 6-16), Plates i (*Frontispiece*); iii, 27, 32; iv, 33; v, 34; coins enclosed in, 34; tendency to ornament in this type, *ib.*; bubbles, or "tears," 33; bowls, ogee and

129

ENGLISH TABLE GLASS

Wine glasses—*continued*.
straight-sided, 51; associated with air-twist stems, *ib.*; of other shape, 53; coloured twist stems (Nos. 101-105), Plate xxiv, 54; rarity of coloured glasses, *ib.*; cut stem (Nos. 106-115), Plates xxv, xxvi, 27, 28, 55, 56; cutting previously employed, probably on larger objects, 55; folded feet, incised twist stems with, probably produced at one early factory, 37, 38; shown in examples presumably from Norwich, 52; folded feet (Nos. 6-12), Plates iii, 32; iv, 33; (Nos. 22-30), Plates vii, 36; viii, 37; (Nos. 58, 91), Plates xv, 44; xxii, 51; incised twist stems, 37; method of manufacture, 38; (Nos. 36-39), Plate x, 39; mixed twists, intermediate links between air twist and spiral, 45; mixed twist not drawn (Nos.

Wine glasses—*continued*.
79-81), Plate xix, 47; plain stems, 34; generally accompanied by folded feet, 35; (Nos. 22-31), Plates vii, viii, 36, 37; Plate i (*Frontispiece*); plain, with domed feet (Nos. 32-35), Plate ix, 38; white twists, how manufactured, 48, 49; method of production analogous to air-twist stems, 49; attributed to Dutch makers, 50; possibly common to both countries, 51; (Nos. 82-100), Plates xx, 48; xxi, 50; xxii, 51; xxiii, 52

YARD-OF-ALE glass. *See* Ale glasses

"Young Pretender." *See* Jacobites

ZOUCHE, SIR EDWARD, alluded to, 23

Zuyder Zee, the, alluded to, 67

THE END

www.ingramcontent.com/pod-product-compliance
Lightning Source LLC
Chambersburg PA
CBHW070644160426
43194CB00009B/1572